POWER WITH PURPOSE

Christians often think about expressions of love or gender roles within marriage. But we overlook the use of power in marriage. However, if our marriage impacts us more than any other human relationship, it is essential for us to consider how to use influence in a God-honoring way. In *Power with Purpose*, David and Krista take you on a biblical exploration of this neglected subject. If you take the time to read it, you'll become more intentional and Christlike in the way you use influence within your marriage.

—**Brad Hambrick**, Pastor of Counseling, The Summit Church, Durham, North Carolina; Author, *Making Sense of Forgiveness: Moving from Hurt Toward Hope*

While reaffirming the beauty of traditional marital roles, David and Krista Dunham provide an incredible service to the church by showing that marriage is about much more than roles. And in a culture filled with reactions and overreactions, *Power with Purpose* is a breath of fresh air that both highlights God's good design for authority and provides a gracious path forward when that God-given authority is misused.

—**Scott Mehl**, Pastor, Cornerstone Church, West Los Angeles; Author, *Redeeming Sex in Marriage*

This is the book I've been waiting for. The Dunhams masterfully frame power as neither a vice to be abandoned nor a privilege to lord over our spouses. Instead, they call us to the beautifully biblical concept of "power with purpose." This Christlike model, rooted in serving and sacrificing for our families out of reverence for the Lord, is the transformative message every marriage needs today.

—**Chris Moles**, Pastor, The Chapel, Eleanor, West Virginia; Author, *The Heart of Domestic Abuse*

Power with Purpose is not just a book about marriage roles—it's a heart-level call to love like Jesus. David and Krista Dunham help us see that biblical authority is not about control but about Christlike sacrifice. With theological clarity and pastoral compassion, they offer a vision of marriage that is rooted in mutual flourishing rather than power struggles. This book is a needed recalibration for couples, churches, and anyone longing to see grace shape the deepest relationships in their lives.

—**Darby Strickland**, Faculty, Christian Counseling & Educational Foundation; Author, *Is It Abuse?* and *When It's Trauma*

Power with Purpose is a theologically grounded and pastorally wise resource that exposes the misplaced trust and self-reliance that are often underneath our craving for control. With Scripture as its foundation and Christ as its aim, this book helps believers pursue true transformation through repentance, humility, and faith in the sovereign grace of God. A valuable counseling tool.

—**Paul Tautges**, Pastor, Cornerstone Community Church, Cleveland, Ohio; Counselor; Author, *Remade* and *Anxiety*

POWER WITH PURPOSE

God's Design for Power Dynamics in Marriage

David R. Dunham &
Krista Dunham

P.O. BOX 817 • PHILLIPSBURG • NEW JERSEY 08865-0817

P&R Publishing offers special discount rates for bulk orders and ministry purchases. To inquire about a special rate, please write to us at sales@prpbooks.com.

Italics within Scripture quotations indicate emphasis added.

Cover design by Jelena Mirkovic

Printed in the United States of America

Library of Congress Cataloging-in-Publication Data

Names: Dunham, David R. author | Dunham, Krista author
Title: Power with purpose : God's design for power dynamics in marriage / David R. Dunham, Krista Dunham.
Description: Phillipsburg, New Jersey : P&R Publishing, [2025] | Summary: "God designed husbands and wives to bring influence, strength, and purpose to their union. Biblical counselors Dave and Krista help spouses to understand their power, then use it for the other's flourishing"-- Provided by publisher.
Identifiers: LCCN 2025032722 | ISBN 9781629952178 paperback | ISBN 9781629953410 epub
Subjects: LCSH: Marriage--Religious aspects--Christianity | Power (Christian theology)
Classification: LCC BV835 .D855 2025
LC record available at https://lccn.loc.gov/2025032722

To
Jacklyn Snider,
Lauren Whitman,
Anne Fletcher,
and Tim Lane

Thank you for showing us
how to display godly power
in our marriage
so that we might help others
learn to live it out in their own

CONTENTS

INTRODUCTION

Have you ever looked for Christian resources on marriage, only to be completely overwhelmed by the sheer abundance of information that is available on the subject? Clearly, Christians care very deeply about marriage, as they should. From our perspective, however, many resources on this topic portray the roles of husbands and wives so narrowly that the primary question they end up answering for couples is "Which one of us is in charge?" Because they keep answering this question, many Christians miss whole portions of God's glorious plan for marriage.

The central focus these resources place on authority, submission, and hierarchy is far more damaging than most people realize. There is a better way to discuss the distribution of power within Christian marriages. What if God designed both husbands and wives to bring real influence, strength, and purpose into their union—not just through structured roles but in a dynamic partnership that uniquely reflects each spouse's contribution? This book explores that concept, inviting you to see marriage not only as a structure but as a shared calling—one in which both husband and wife possess power for the purpose of helping each other flourish.

You may have picked up this book while seeking to strengthen an already healthy marriage. Maybe you want your marriage to have purpose and direction. We hope to show you how a bad view of power can lead even good marriages to miss out on God's best. Or you may be experiencing conflict with your spouse due to a power struggle or a misunderstanding of marriage roles. We give guidance from Scripture that may help you resolve those issues and restore health to your relationship.

One particular dynamic that we are burdened to speak about is the type of power struggle that leads to abuse. While many great resources help readers recognize and address abuse directly, our overall desire in this book is to address power problems before they turn into abuse. Power is a valuable and gracious gift that God has given to couples; we hope to provide information that will help husbands and wives use power in the way that God designed it to be used.

CHANGE FOR INDIVIDUALS

If you were to ask married couples within any modern evangelical church to explain the biblical roles of godly husbands and wives, they would most likely answer with two simple words: *headship* and *submission*. Some pastors and teachers would see this as evidence that evangelicals are winning the battle against male apathy and female dominance, which they believe have threatened to destroy God's purpose for the church and for marriage. But others, especially those whose eyes have been opened to domestic abuse cases within the church, conclude that these answers are problematic.

What usually lies behind such answers is an unbiblical view of leadership. Young men are often taught principles that elevate authority and neglect sacrifice. This gives them reason to pursue control and dominance above love, understanding, and service. They overemphasize their position of leadership to such an extent that their marriages cease to be partnerships and devolve into dictatorships. Conversely, young women are frequently given so many applications of submission that they lose all sense of agency within their marriages. When a wife doesn't learn to speak the truth in love or develop a discerning mind and a courageous spirit, the positive influence she could have on her husband fades into the background. Focusing on submission alone diminishes the actual role she is meant to fulfill as helper.

We are passionate about addressing power dynamics in marriage because of our experience as counselors. Wives have come to us feeling crushed, silenced, and trapped by an unhealthy interpretation of submission. They often express a loss of identity, dignity, and purpose within their marriages. Meanwhile, their husbands feel anxious, overwhelmed, and confused about what it even means to be a "spiritual leader" in the home. Both spouses are perpetually struggling to function under a weight that they were never meant to carry alone or, in some cases, at all. Wives struggle to be heard without nagging or to be humble without becoming a doormat. Husbands struggle to find a balance between passivity and tyranny. They all need clarity and help.

Our need for clarity regarding power dynamics in marriage is dire. Without this clarity, we face real dangers. In our own ministry, we have seen a considerable rise in the number of Christian men who are misusing their God-given role by bullying and abusing their wives. These men have come into our offices as active church members. They know Scripture well but use it as a weapon against their wives. They are not using their leadership for the good of anyone but themselves, looking only to achieve their own desired outcomes. Wives call us terrified and confused after their husbands use the Bible to shame or mistreat them in terrible ways. Wives in these situations feel helpless, especially when they seek solace in their churches only to be told, "You must submit." Something has to happen on an individual level so that marriages can thrive and flourish as God intended.

OUR EXPERIENCE IN MARRIAGE

Our own marital experience informs our approach to this topic as well. In many ways we are writing the book we wish we had read at the start of our marriage. We are one of those couples that we mentioned in previous paragraphs. Engaged at nineteen with plans to pursue ministry together, we immediately began exploring what God had to say about marriage. We wanted to do our best to get it right. Not really even knowing how to study the Bible properly, we heavily relied on other resources for the answers we needed to form the foundation of our married life. We wanted so badly to please God in our relationship that we devoured an extensive amount of content very quickly.

It wasn't long before we developed pretty strong convictions about how our marriage should function. Though we learned that a husband was given authority and a wife was called to submit to him, that was the extent of the biblical truth that shaped our marital worldview. The remaining truths that we lived by came from the illustrations and examples that various authors and teachers presented as they described how those principles of Scripture should be lived out. So much of what we did focused on making sure the world around us was aware that our relationship was different. That difference, however, was demonstrated not by loving each other well but by emphasizing who was in charge. Perhaps you can relate to some of the ways in which we conceptualized power dynamics in our marriage:

> I should drop everything I am doing to greet him when he gets home because he deserves my attention and respect.
>
> If she is not consistently getting the dishes done, the right thing for me to do is to confront her about that. If I just did them myself, I would be undermining the authority I am supposed to have over her.
>
> I really think it's a bad idea for us to move right now, but it would be ungodly and disobedient for me to disagree with my husband—God will bless me for submitting to him without question.
>
> I know my wife has a lot more experience and gifting in the area of finances, but since I'm the head of this household, I need to be in charge of all our money—God will bless our endeavors simply because I have stepped up and taken leadership.

We spent nearly two decades of marriage operating under similar principles. We made hundreds of choices based on the framework that marriage is simply the exercise of male headship and female submission. Our story played out like that of many other Christian couples who build their marriages on a similar framework: The husband was to make the final decisions, which meant he could veto any options that he didn't think were best, while also establishing any new options that he found important. So, even though the wife could offer her input, the husband's authority basically rendered it obsolete anyway. The wife was to operate under the assumption that her husband knew what was best for her and that he was making decisions for the good of them both. She did this by never questioning his motives, by being careful and calculated regarding when and if she shared her input, and by acknowledging that he was wise and driven by his intellect whereas she was easily given to emotion and temptation. His decisions could lead her to do any number of things: transfer the kids to a different school, buy a new car, or pack everything up and spend the rest of her life without seeing her family ever again—it didn't matter. The godliest thing for him to do was to exert his authority, and the godliest thing for her to do was to submit to the authority that he was exerting.

Our marriage experienced something of a snowball effect—though, in the aftermath, we might have described it as an avalanche. What started out as a small crack in the foundation nearly brought our relationship toppling down. Within our marriage, Dave's opinion was viewed as more valuable than Krista's, which gradually led us to operate as if Dave had all the answers and was always right. Out of that, Dave developed more and more pride, and Krista became more and more trepidatious, so the problem grew and grew over time. Over twenty years, that seemingly insignificant mistake morphed into a vital error.

We have both described our experience to each other in a similar way: God brought us right to the very edge of the worst thing that could have happened to our marriage relationship, only to snatch us back at the last moment. Through this struggle we found the motivation to reexamine Scripture and develop a crucial understanding of what marriage should really be about. The time we spent at the edge has helped us see that marriage has a whole lot less to do with who is in charge and a whole lot more to do with love. This seems so obvious to say, and yet it is so frequently missed.

In our attempt to put authority and submission above everything, we made a lot of assumptions about what God would bless and what would displease him. Much of our thinking was based on information that wasn't even in the Bible. We essentially assumed that God would bless a wife for overlooking her husband's sin just because she was diligent to acknowledge his authority and, likewise, that God would bless a husband for being foolish as long as he was diligent to take the lead. This sums up the irrationality of reducing individual marital roles to mere hierarchy when teaching husbands and wives how to live. There is only one command in Scripture that stands to get that much attention, and it is not about authority or submission. It is about love.

We would have been spared a lot of heartache in our marriage if we had given that much attention to love. We wouldn't have needed to seek our own ways of getting or keeping power. Dave wouldn't have run with the power he had, using his leadership as a means to get more. He wouldn't have gotten defensive when he felt that his authority was being threatened. Krista wouldn't have viciously clung to the small areas where it seemed that her power mattered. She wouldn't have spiraled into depression when she felt invisible and forgotten, thinking, "Maybe God just loves him more than he loves me." We wouldn't have devised little ways to exert power when we felt that we had none. We wouldn't have made decisions to benefit our own ambitions and desires. We would have sought to see and hear the other person instead of attempting to punish them when we weren't seen or heard ourselves.

The biblical use of power gives us an alternative to these approaches. The biblical use of power looks like love. It looks like sacrifice. It looks like putting the other person first so that they can be empowered. It is relinquishing our own need to attain recognition or notoriety. It is rejoicing deep in our hearts at the success and joys of the other, not expecting anything in return—yet having the confidence that we won't be forgotten because we both have made love the foundation.

WHY YOU NEED THIS BOOK

Like us, many couples in the church have been taught about male headship and female submission. They understand that there is some power dynamic at play in marriage, but without proper discipleship they import all sorts of ideas into their conception of power. Most often, these ideas stem from worldly and even harmful uses of power. Our understanding of power is often derived from a Genesis-3 world as opposed to a Genesis-2 world. We mimic what is at play in the world due to the curse of sin rather than working to display God's true desire and purpose for power.

One of the primary principles we can draw from Genesis 2 is that God's intent for husband and wife is oneness. God determined that it is not good for man to be alone—man needs a companion. Then, to demonstrate this need, God parades all the animals in front of Adam, but "for the man no helper was found corresponding to him" (v. 20). God then takes man and from him creates a suitable companion: woman. Sensing how suitable the woman is to him, Adam immediately bursts forth into a song of praise (see v. 23), after which Moses offers us a compelling commentary on the whole event: "This is why a man leaves his father and mother and bonds with his wife, and they become one flesh" (v. 24).

Union, oneness . . . this was God's intent for the marital relationship. That isn't to suggest that headship didn't exist before the fall. Paul indicates that male headship and female submission were also part of God's original intent (see 1 Tim. 2:12–13).[1] But the exercise of that headship was meant to breed unity and mutual flourishing. Likewise, the woman's use of power was originally intended for mutual flourishing. The woman is called a "helper" fit for man. This term is frequently misunderstood, and that misunderstanding is rooted in a larger and more fundamental misunderstanding regarding gender roles.

The original intent behind the teachings of complementarianism[2] was the understanding that the roles of husbands and wives are different in function but equal in value and worth. Often, however, wives still feel less valued and understood within their homes. In part, this feeling of devaluation persists because much of marriage has been reduced to headship and submission. When hierarchy is the only way to describe the husband–wife dynamic, then a husband can make decisions that bring him great personal gain and be praised for "leading his family well." Meanwhile, his wife will be reprimanded if she struggles in any way to comply with her husband's "leadership." And so *helper* becomes synonymous with *assistant* or *servant* rather than portraying the mutuality for which it was intended.

1. In this text Paul grounds his argument for male-only church eldership on the fact that man was created before woman. We believe the phrase "have authority" concerns eldership and not all instruction, encouragement, or even teaching done by women. A related passage, 1 Corinthians 14:32–35, deals with the subject of women teaching authoritatively. We know that Paul welcomed women prophesying in church, so the idea that it is "disgraceful for a woman to speak in the church" must mean something more specific. We would contend that it refers to authoritative teaching via the office of elder or pastor.

2. Complementarianism is a particular theological approach to understanding gender roles in marriage, church, and society. It was first developed by the Council on Biblical Manhood and Womanhood.

Instruction given to a husband should include teaching him to notice his wife's longings, to empathize with her struggles (see 1 Peter 3:7), and to empower her to grow spiritually and personally. His role as leader does not guarantee he gets what he wants; rather, it allows him to use his power and position to serve his wife and build her up. His authority is given not so that he can lord it over her but as a means of lifting her up and helping her flourish.

Likewise, rather than making submission the primary focus of a wife's role, we can better describe her position by the word *helper*. *Helper* is a more accurate description of a wife's role because it was the word that God used to describe Eve when he gave her to Adam. God created woman because the man needed her help. God had a plan that required two genders instead of one to reflect himself within the world and to accomplish his great purposes. And, as we will go on to demonstrate, *helper* is a better description of a wife's role because it forms an umbrella under which all other responsibilities of a wife fall. *Submission* does not fully describe all aspects of what a wife is supposed to do, but it can be one way that a wife helps her husband.

Both of these descriptions more effectively portray the concepts of care and responsibility that we all should have toward one another as coheirs in the kingdom of God. And this, in turn, gives us a more robust understanding of both spouses' relationship to power within their marriage. A wife should focus not solely on submission but also on the influence she has within her marriage. As a helper, she focuses on strengthening, sustaining, and sharpening her husband. A husband should focus not solely on his authority but on providing support, safety, and stability in all areas of marriage. Together they focus on the goals God has given them collectively as they mutually submit to and sacrifice for each other. As they seek to honor God in this way and practically fulfill these responsibilities, they can provide better means for flourishing within their families, churches, and communities.

Nearly every book on marriage talks about marital roles. It has been our experience, though, that most don't talk about them from a *robust* biblical perspective. They reduce these roles simply to headship and submission. They leave out important balancing terms and instructions and thus fail to put the proper emphasis on love. And that sort of reduction leads to confusion and harm, resulting in the spike of abuse within Christian marriages. That is why we need one more book on marriage.

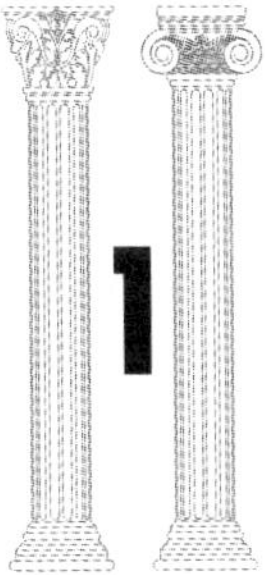

1 UNDERSTANDING POWER

In 1099 the city of Jerusalem was captured by the first Crusaders. What followed was the slaughter of nearly thirty thousand Jewish and Muslim inhabitants of the city in two days. The Crusades are often identified as one of the worst atrocities committed in the name of Christ. To say, then, that Christians have a strange and complex relationship with power would be an understatement. On the one hand, Jesus taught that the "meek" (NIV) or "humble" are "blessed" (Matt. 5:5). He taught us to turn the other cheek and to "pray for those who persecute" us (Matt. 5:39, 44). This seems to suggest that we should avoid the pursuit of power. And yet power is required to make something of the world.[1] The Lord gave power to humanity and called them to exercise dominion over the creation (see Gen. 1:26–28). And, as we will see, there are different types of power given to people in different roles. Power is a part of life.

1. See Andy Crouch, *Playing God: Redeeming the Gift of Power* (IVP, 2013), 17.

Power has the potential to devastate, but it also has the potential to bless. It is important, then, that we think about power—particularly our use of power within the home. After all, just as power exists within the world, so it exists within marriage. All marriages have power dynamics. If we understand and use power rightly, it can lead to tremendous flourishing within the marital relationship and for each spouse individually. If we misunderstand and misuse power, however, it can have devastating consequences.

According to Scripture, power has a purpose. That purpose concerns not merely our capacities and capabilities but also the end for which those capacities and capabilities are used. Power was never intended to be used for personal gain. It was given to us by God in order to serve others, uphold justice, and reflect God's character in the world. Scripture consistently presents power as the ability to support others so they can grow, thrive, and live in alignment with God's design. In short, the goal of power is to help others flourish. That is the purpose of power, both in the world and in the home.

THE ORIGIN & DEFINITION OF POWER

The word *power* refers simply to the ability to do something. We can have power in the form of influence, control, or strength. We can have physical, social, or even mechanical power. We have the ability to maintain or hold together existing realities, or we have the ability to change those realities. A person can be powerful, an organization can be powerful, an engine can be powerful.

Relational power—which is what we are considering in this book—refers to the ability to influence, guide, or affect another person. This form of power comes into play when one individual uses their personal strength, position, privilege, or resources to influence, guide, and affect others. Such power can be used, as we will see, positively or negatively depending on the nature of the relationship and the individuals involved in it.

Before we talk about how power can be misused and how that misuse impacts us, it's important for us to first understand what Scripture says about power itself. The Bible teaches that all authority ultimately comes from God. Romans 13:1 reminds us, "There is no authority except from God, and the authorities that exist are instituted by God." In other words, God is the one who places people in positions of authority. Colossians 1:16 expands this idea even further: "For everything was created by [Jesus], in heaven and on earth, the visible and the invisible, whether thrones or dominions or rulers or authorities—all things have been created through him and for him." God is the only true source of power. All other power is just an outflow of that source.

So, power is not something humans generate—it is given, not earned or created. But when God gives power, his own source is never depleted, because any power someone else holds is simply a portion entrusted to them by him. Because God created all things, including systems of authority, he alone determines how power is distributed. As Job 12:23 puts it, "He makes nations great, then destroys them." Everything is subject to his wisdom and rule.

Although God gives more power to some than to others, Scripture also makes it clear that God is the ultimate authority and that he does not show any partiality. Just because one person has more power than another does not win them favor with God. Both slave and master on earth have the same Master in heaven (see Eph. 6:9). Both prisoner and jailer look heavenward for mercy. Both teacher and student look to the Bible for truth. And, as we will discuss in more detail later, both wife and husband answer to the same authority. This also means that in order to maintain wise and godly authority, the one who has been given power must look to the Lord for wisdom. Yet even those who don't acknowledge God are still subject to his authority. As Proverbs 21:1 says, "A king's heart is like channeled water in the LORD's hand: He directs it wherever he chooses."

Authority requires responsibility, but God has ultimate control.

POWER'S PURPOSE & OUR GREAT EXAMPLE

If power is given by God, then we know it can be good. Yet to experience the benefits of power, we must think of it differently from the world around us. Jesus teaches us how to do this when he contrasts power in the kingdom of God with power in the world.

> You know that the rulers of the Gentiles lord it over them, and those in high positions act as tyrants over them. It must not be like that among you. On the contrary, whoever wants to become great among you must be your servant, and whoever wants to be first among you must be your slave; just as the Son of Man did not come to be served, but to serve, and to give his life as a ransom for many. (Matt. 20:25–28)

Jesus taught his disciples this on an occasion when James and John (through their mother) were vying for special authority and power in the coming kingdom of God. Jesus showed all the disciples that power in God's kingdom is intended to be used to serve others. Those who don't know God (the Gentiles) use power to "lord it over" others—to dominate and rule them. It is not, however, supposed to be that way among Jesus's followers. They are to imitate their Lord, our great example. Though he is God, Jesus came not be served but to use his power to serve others.

This distinction between "lording" over and serving is the difference between power that is used to oppress and power that is used to help others flourish. We talk about it using the language of *power over* and *power under.*[2]

Those who practice *power over* elevate self and personal agenda by oppressing others. They push people down to make them and their strengths subservient to their desires. Someone who seeks *power over* may be physically harmful—abusive in the classic sense of the word—or simply dismissive of others. They may be critical, insulting, harsh, and manipulative. Others may simply think that their agendas are more important, their needs more urgent, their wants and preferences more significant. They do not necessarily intend to harm others, but their self-focus still leads to that result.

Those who pursue *power under*, in contrast, elevate others and serve their needs, concerns, and desires. They identify the strengths of others and help them cultivate those strengths. They desire to help their spouses flourish. They listen to the concerns of others, consider their interests, and make decisions based on benefiting them, not only benefiting self.

Pastor and counselor Chris Moles depicts *power under* with a helpful illustration from the world of cheerleading:

> Consider college cheerleaders, in particular the male cheerleaders, as an illustration of power under. During a college football or basketball game you will often see the female cheerleaders performing amazing athletic feats such as flips or demonstrating tremendous balance while leading cheers high above the turf or court. While our attention is on the female

2. This is language that we have adopted from our dear friend Chris Moles.

> cheerleaders, her ability to be seen or to be given the space to perform those amazing feats is due in part to the male cheerleader's strength. Her ability and skill are on display because of his tremendous strength and dependability. . . . In much the same way, we husbands are to use our power to support, protect, and communicate that we too are dependable and responsible with the power we have been given.[3]

Power under means using our power and leadership to help others flourish and use their skills and gifts well. It follows the model of Jesus, whose whole life and ministry was an act of service. The incarnation itself shows how Christ used his power for the good of others. Paul tells us this plainly.

> Adopt the same attitude as that of Christ Jesus,
> who, existing in the form of God,
> did not consider equality with God
> as something to be exploited. Instead he emptied himself
> by assuming the form of a servant,
> taking on the likeness of humanity.
> And when he had come as a man,
> he humbled himself by becoming obedient
> to the point of death—
> even to death on a cross. (Phil. 2:5–8)

As God, Jesus had every right not to involve himself in our brokenness. He had all power and could exercise it however he pleased. His response to our need, however, was to lay down his

3. Chris Moles, *The Heart of Domestic Abuse: Gospel Solutions for Men Who Use Control and Violence in the Home* (Focus, 2015), 73.

nobility and to sacrifice himself for our good. He used his power not to gain anything for himself but to give up something invaluable in order to gain for us full spiritual flourishing. He died so that we might live eternally in the presence of our Father in heaven. The incarnation is a powerful act, but it is a powerful act to serve others. Jesus uses his power to help others flourish.

From the very beginning, even before the incarnation, this was how human beings were to use our power. In fact, it was God's intention even in the garden of Eden. In Genesis 2, God entrusted mankind with authority—not for self-interest but for stewardship and service. God gave Adam the responsibility to cultivate and protect the garden, and he created Eve as Adam's necessary counterpart for sharing in the task of bringing life and flourishing to creation. Their authority was meant to reflect God's own rule—marked by care, provision, and love. But when sin entered the world, power became distorted; instead of using it for the good of others, fallen humans began to wield it for control and selfish gain. This broken use of power led to strife, division, and exploited relationships. Yet Jesus restored the original design by demonstrating that true power is found not in dominance but in humility, sacrifice, and love. In him, we see that the greatest authority is exercised not by lording it over others but by lifting them up and seeking their good.

Jesus is our example, and we are called to imitate him. Just hours before his betrayal and crucifixion, Jesus gathered his disciples—not to command them but to serve them. He washed their feet, a task reserved for the lowest servant. What is striking about this passage is how John introduces it. He connects Jesus's acts of service to his power.

> Jesus knew that the Father had given everything into his hands, that he had come from God, and that he was going back to

> God. So he got up from supper, laid aside his outer clothing, took a towel, and tied it around himself. Next, he poured water into a basin and began to wash his disciples' feet and to dry them with the towel tied around him. (John 13:3–5)

It was precisely *because* Jesus held all power that he was able to serve with such humility. He directed his power to achieve the good of others. In the face of his impending death, he did not use his power to gather his forces or strengthen his defense. Instead, he used it to wash the disciples' feet. If this is how Christ used his power, then as his followers, we are called to do the same, both in our individual lives and within our marriages. Power—whether in leadership or influence—is not about control but about serving, uplifting, and encouraging one another.

In helping us understand the significance of this event, John says that Jesus had all things under his power, that he was from God and returning to God. Jesus has power; indeed, he has ultimate power—that is, divine power. How does this all-powerful God-man use it? He gets up from the meal, wraps a towel around his waist, and washes dirty feet. He serves others.

And when he has done this, Jesus teaches us to imitate him, again connecting service to power.

> When Jesus had washed their feet and put on his outer clothing, he reclined again and said to them, "Do you know what I have done for you? You call me Teacher and Lord—and you are speaking rightly, since that is what I am. So if I, your Lord and Teacher, have washed your feet, you also ought to wash one another's feet. For I have given you an example, that you also should do just as I have done for you.
>
> "Truly I tell you, a servant is not greater than his master,

> and a messenger is not greater than the one who sent him.
> If you know these things, you are blessed if you do them."
> (vv. 12–17)

Jesus reminds us that he has performed this act of service as Lord. If our Master used his power to serve, then we too must use all our power to serve others. No one is above "washing feet." Power in God's kingdom is all about serving others such that they flourish and thrive. Jesus models this service and calls us to it as well.

If we want to imitate Christ, then we must recognize that we have a responsibility to help others flourish. It's not merely that we want others to succeed in life and faith, though we should want that. Imitating Christ, being his followers, obligates us to use our power for service. This is his way, and this is what power in his kingdom looks like. "I have given you an example," he says, "that you also should do just as I have done for you."

Using power to help others flourish means that we use our strength, influence, assets, privileges, positions, and more so that others will thrive. We imitate Christ by laying down our rights in order to meet someone else's needs. Practically, this may mean that we recognize the power of our own voice in a conversation, and, instead of dominating the conversation or ending it when our ideas have been heard, we give space for others to comment or share their ideas. Maybe it means giving someone else a chance to work on a project, even when we know that they won't do it the way we would. Perhaps it means providing people who have limited resources with the supplies and amenities that they need to fulfill their own dreams, visions, or plans. Sometimes it may mean completely sacrificing our own desires because what we want is not best for everyone involved. There are countless ways to use our power to help others; in each scenario we have the opportunity to imitate Jesus.

Power always has the potential, regardless of circumstances, to cause harm or promote flourishing. You may understand this on a personal level if you have ever experienced the difference between a cruel boss and an inspiring one. For a business to operate efficiently, someone has to be in charge, but the outcome is determined by whether the person in authority chooses to use their power for good or for evil. Bosses can inspire employees to work their hardest by encouraging and respecting them, or they can intentionally exploit and overwork those who are under them. When bosses choose to benefit themselves by misusing power, they are the only ones who stand to gain. It is difficult for the other individuals or the system as a whole to succeed in these conditions. The workers become despondent and frustrated, which leads to less respect and productivity overall. In contrast, using power to help others flourish has a positive impact on the entire system and on anyone who relies on that system.

What is true of power in the workforce is also true of power in a marriage. When it is used selfishly, it can only bring about minimal personal benefit while causing harm to anyone else who might be affected. But when it used sacrificially, it can cause the individuals, the relationship, and everyone who interacts with them to experience its benefits. Using power for good, rather than evil, brings about the most flourishing for the most people.

CAUTIONS ABOUT POWER

Although the world highlights the benefits of possessing power, the Bible encourages us to also contemplate its challenges and responsibilities. The Bible says that those who are in authority must give an account to God on behalf of those under them (see Heb. 13:17). Those who seek positions of authority, especially within the church, are held to higher standards. They must be more attentive to building their character. They must be more cautious to avoid temptation. They must live in such a way as to be an example to those they lead (see 1 Peter 5:3). Husbands are not to be harsh with their wives (see Col. 3:19), and fathers are not to provoke their children (see Eph. 6:4). Uncle Ben was right when he said, "With great power comes great responsibility."[4] Many people seek after power and fight for it because they want to be able to achieve their goals or be treated with respect. When authority or power falls into your possession, it is important to also think of the responsibility that comes along with it.

The Bible warns us against the allure of power. Even pastors are not immune from its clutches. Those in authority over the church can become greedy for their own gain or puffed up with conceit (see 1 Tim. 3). In times of chaos, the church will not succeed at the things it is called to do if people put themselves first and fail to honor the authority that God has established (see 3 John 1:9–10). We are told, in fact, that it is God's power that is made perfect through our weakness (see 2 Cor. 12:9). We are meant to be weak so that God's strength can take center stage. When we try to unduly magnify our own power, God will lovingly find a way to bring us down so that we don't pridefully and dangerously attempt to take his glory for ourselves.

Jesus is our ultimate example, and he laid his life down for those over whom he had authority. The least we can do is to lay aside our own desires and reputations for the advantage of those God has put within our care. In following Jesus, we learn that

4. *Spider-Man*, directed by Sam Raimi, Sony Pictures, 2002.

having authority does not mean getting our own way (see Eph. 5:25). Power requires that we give of ourselves so that others might benefit.

THE MISUSE OF POWER

Although God intended for us to use our power for the good of others, sadly, we often use it to benefit ourselves. Power today is frequently viewed with skepticism and cynicism, and we can readily understand why. Sin leads many to use power for selfish gain. Writer and orator Robert Ingersoll said, "If you want to know what a man is to the bottom, give him power. Any man can stand adversity—only a great man can stand prosperity."[5] It is true that you will see a person's character most clearly on display when they are handed a measure of power. Often, greater power magnifies this reality. It is dangerous to give someone power because there is always a chance that they will not use it properly.

By definition, power involves other people, and so when power is abused, innocent people are often abused in the process. This tragic reality is nowhere more painful or personal than in the marriage relationship, where misused power can wound the very person it was meant to protect and cherish.

The misuse of power in marriage occurs when one or both spouses exercise their God-given influence in ways that depart from its intended design. Remember, at its core, power is the capacity to shape the thoughts, choices, or direction of another person. In a healthy relationship, this capacity is exercised in alignment with love, justice, and mutual honor. Misuse, however, bends that capacity toward ends that do not reflect God's heart. It

5. Robert G. Ingersoll, *Abraham Lincoln: A Lecture* (New York, 1895), 15.

distorts authority and responsibility, twisting them from means of service into instruments of self-interest.

Defining the misuse of power requires us to understand the legitimate purpose of power. Power in marriage is meant to be relationally constructive—to uphold commitments, strengthen trust, and foster mutual flourishing. When power is used in a way that undermines these purposes, it moves from being a blessing to being a curse. This shift is often subtle in its beginnings but perilous in its trajectory, as it reorients the relationship away from partnership toward control or neglect.

The misuse of power in marriage can take many forms, but it is always characterized by a misalignment between purpose and practice. The one who wields power may still possess the same position or ability as before, but the posture of their heart has shifted from stewardship to selfishness. It is this internal reorientation—rather than the mere presence of power—that transforms an otherwise neutral capacity into one that is misused. Such misuse may not always be obvious, yet it consistently deviates from the standard of God-honoring love.

A key element in identifying misuse is recognizing that all marital power is inherently relational. Power in marriage is not an isolated force but is bound up in the covenantal connection between two people. Because of this, its misuse cannot be separated from its intimate and covenantal context. This makes the stewardship of power uniquely significant: How it is exercised will either reflect or betray the sacred trust of the marriage covenant.

At the heart of the misuse of power in marriage is a failure to reflect the servant-hearted character of Christ. In the biblical vision, power is never an end in itself but is entrusted for the good of another. Whenever it departs from this design, it ceases to be the good gift it was intended to be. Understanding this reality lays the groundwork for examining how power, when mishandled, can undermine the covenant rather than uphold it.

THE IMPACT OF MISUSED POWER

Many people have come to accept misused power as a normal part of everyday life. Some even believe that power is *supposed* to be misused. Unfortunately, we are so often led to believe that angry, dominating personalities are required for leadership that we can feel surprised to have a pleasant, supportive boss who is looking out for our good.

Romantic relationships can have a similar dynamic. Our media often portrays manipulation and coercion in marriage as humorous, normal, or even justified, rather than wrong or even unhealthy. In sitcoms, guilt-trips, silent treatment, or emotional blackmail are treated as gags rather than harmful practices. The clever wife outsmarts the clueless husband, or the cunning husband tricks his unsuspecting wife into letting him do what he wants—all for the sake of getting laughs. This makes coercion seem harmless or even expected in relationships.

These behaviors become such a regular part of our media consumption, even for Christians, that they don't set off any red flags when we see them appear in our own relationships. Rather than pursuing honesty and healthy communication, couples believe manipulation and coercion are necessary to get what they want. A proper understanding of power will see these as harmful to relational health and sinful before the Lord.

On its own, misused power has the potential to greatly harm a victim because it touches on every aspect of their human experience. The misappropriation of God's good gift of power can be physically, emotionally, and spiritually traumatic because it affects the mind, the soul, and the body.

Misused Power Impacts the Emotions

When power is used against someone or handled in an unhealthy way, the victim may experience a sense of helplessness and anxiety that comes from being stripped of their safety, dignity, agency, and voice. An atmosphere of fear and instability results.

A spouse who is being harmed by misused power feels trapped and controlled by someone who should have been a source of guidance and care. Betrayal by a spouse causes emotional distress because it shatters trust, making it difficult to feel secure in the relationship. The wounded may question their ability to judge character and discern situations rightly. The emotional turmoil can lead to anger and resentment, particularly when justice is denied or when the perpetrator remains in the position of power.

The abuse of power often leads to shame and self-doubt as victims internalize their suffering, wondering if they were at fault or if they deserved the mistreatment they received. Victims can become depressed and self-condemning; they may even experience intense despair, especially if they can see no way out of the situation. Healing from such an experience requires more than just time—it demands the restoration of trust, justice, and a reaffirmation of one's inherent value as an image bearer of God.

Jake and Lana had been married for seven years when she started to notice that he had been asserting control over most areas of their life together: how they spent their money, who they spent time with, and even how she expressed her emotions. When she tried to tell him how she felt, he said, "You're always so sensitive! If you really loved me, you wouldn't question me." When

Lana tried to express her needs by asking him to help with the kids, Jake replied, "I work hard all day. You don't even appreciate me, or you would know how tired I am." If she tried to talk with him about a circumstance in which he had sinned against her, he said, "You always make me out to be the bad guy." He would flip any issues back on her, and the conversation would end with her feeling confused and defeated.

Lana gradually became more and more emotionally exhausted by their relationship. She felt as if she had to walk on eggshells when they were home together. But when she was away from him, she found herself worrying about his next assertion of power. Lana's emotional health deteriorated as she felt unheard, unseen, and invalidated. She began to experience anxiety and a deep sense of isolation. Even though she was married, she felt completely alone. Jake's misuse of power left her feeling trapped, questioning her own worth and afraid to speak up for herself.

Misused Power Impacts Spiritual Health

Scripture reveals God to be a defender of the oppressed, and it tells us that true authority should reflect his justice, mercy, and love. The misuse of power often leads people to wrestle with God's presence in the midst of their suffering. They might even question why he would allow such injustice to occur. In particular, it can lead people to associate abusive power with the God who controls all things and who is all-powerful. The misuse of spiritual truths in order to gain power and control over another often distorts a person's understanding of God, leaving them confused about his character and whether he truly cares for them. A person can be led to doubt, disillusionment, and even a crisis of faith.

Many victims of spiritual abuse struggle with guilt, shame, and fear because they have been manipulated into believing that obedience to an oppressive spouse equals obedience to God. This can make it difficult for them to approach God with trust and confidence. Some may turn away from faith entirely, associating God with the corruption of those who claimed to represent him. Others may develop a works-based or fear-driven spirituality, feeling they must earn their worth or avoid punishment. In some cases, people remain in harmful environments, believing they are being tested by God or that suffering under unjust spouses is a form of spiritual virtue. Healing from the spiritual damage caused by an abuse of power often requires rediscovering God's true nature—one of grace, protection, and care for the brokenhearted (see Ps. 34:18).

We can turn to the Bible to see a clear example of what such spiritual damage looks like. The Pharisees used their authority to burden the people of Israel with oppressive religious rules while excusing their own hypocrisy. Jesus condemned them harshly, calling them "whitewashed tombs" (Matt. 23:27) because they appeared righteous on the outside but were corrupt on the inside. The people who followed their teaching became emotionally and spiritually exhausted as they were manipulated into believing their worth depended on rule-keeping rather than on God's grace.

These types of situations aren't limited to scriptural or even religious contexts. Many people who have grown up in legalistic or authoritarian environments or who have struggled under a spouse's misuse of power may understand the shame, fear, and distrust that burdened the disciples of the Pharisees. The instructions and training that come out of these harsh environments often lead people to abandon the faith altogether. From a spiritual perspective, the effects of misused power can be incredibly devastating. The victim may not just be physically and emotionally impacted here and now, but their soul can be eternally affected if they choose to walk away from God. This is why power of any type should be thoughtfully considered and guarded with the utmost caution. It should never be taken lightly.

Misused Power Impacts the Body

Even when power doesn't directly produce noticeable marks on a body, it can still have serious physical effects on victims as they experience persistent pressure and emotional stress. Chronic anxiety and fear can lead to increased levels of stress hormones, which weakens the immune system and makes a person more vulnerable to sickness. Due to the body's prolonged state of fight-or-flight, sufferers of abuse can experience headaches, digestive issues, muscle tension, and fatigue. Sleep disturbances, including insomnia or nightmares, are common, as victims struggle to feel safe and at peace.

In severe cases, the physical impact can escalate to high blood pressure, heart disease, or other stress-related conditions. As they attempt to manage emotional pain, some victims may also develop unhealthy coping mechanisms, like substance abuse, self-harm, or disordered eating.

The body and the mind are deeply connected, so that when power is used to control, oppress, or harm, the physical consequences are directly linked to the emotional wounds. Some of these physical issues end up being attributed to other common factors so that blame is never directed toward the actual perpetrator. This can keep a victim stuck in a cycle of harm because the problem is misdiagnosed.

Mark and Rachel are a prime example of what happens when misused power takes a physical toll.[6] Rachel had always known

6. Many of the examples in this book will reflect on the male misuse of power. There will be discussions of a woman's misuse of power as well, but

that Mark was a little controlling, but when they were dating it didn't seem like that big of a deal. Now that they are approaching their tenth anniversary, she is trying to remember what it felt like not to be trapped under his leadership.

Rachel used to imagine that Mark was a great spiritual leader. Even in college, he had known his Bible well, and their classmates turned to him for guidance. But what she once admired now feels like a punishment as he lords his knowledge over her and uses it to make her feel small. His ideas on authority and submission seemed a little harsh to her, but it was hard for her to disagree since he could always point directly to Scripture to prove his opinions. They read so many books on marriage that seemed to support his views as well.

Mark has never laid a hand on her, but sometimes she wonders if his actions have caused the pain for which she can't find an answer. The amount of tension she holds in her body on a daily basis cannot be good for her. Her doctor has encouraged her to consider other stress-related factors, but the rest of her life seems pretty relaxed. She loves being a mom to their two kids, she has a good group of Christian friends, and both sides of their family are supportive and helpful. Rachel doesn't feel like there is any way she could confront Mark, and she doesn't know if she even should. She feels trapped and exhausted.

CONCLUSION

Despite the horrific ways that power has been used and abused, power itself is not evil. God gave us power so that we might serve

---

we recognize that God has given men a greater level of power, and therefore they are often more likely to misuse it. Men, bear with us in these examples. Keep reading and see what you can learn.

one another. He models that for us and calls us to imitate him in precisely this manner. Power has a purpose: to help others flourish. That is true of all uses of power, but, as we will see next, it is especially true of the use of power in marriage.

QUESTIONS FOR REFLECTION

1. In what ways have you experienced the misuse of power? What makes the misuse of power so devastating?
2. What might be some benefits of power? Have you witnessed or experienced any of these benefits?
3. Can you think of any other examples of Jesus's use of power for the good of others? How does Jesus's example help you think about power differently?
4. How might this discussion of power, generally, help you to think about the use of power in marriage specifically?

2

POWER IN MARRIAGE

Many young couples are taught that the husband is the head of the home and that wives are called to submit. Bible verses are used to reinforce these principles, and newlyweds are told that this is the most biblically faithful way to live. Most young couples are not, however, given any practical guidance on exactly what that looks like. What do *spiritual headship* and *submission* mean in our day-to-day lives together? As a result of this limited education, many couples have suffered under misguided notions of power in marriage. The reality is that both husbands and wives have their own unique type of power that is to be used for the flourishing of the other.

TYPES OF POWER IN MARRIAGE

Everyone has some kind of power. God gives to humanity the power to rule and exercise dominion over creation (see Gen.

1:28). He has given this power to both man and woman. He has called men and women alike to "subdue" the earth and to "rule" over it.[1] Yet within that broad calling, we find various levels of authority, power, and leadership.

We see, for example, that parents have a unique type of power that their children do not have. Children are called to obey parents and submit to their authority (see Eph. 6:1–3). Likewise, pastors have a certain level of authority within the church. They are unique leaders, and Scripture calls congregations to obey and submit to them (see Heb. 13:17). God has also appointed governments to have authority over their citizens. Scripture calls us to submit to our ruling authorities (see Rom. 13:1). No authority God has given comes with complete control, nor does any submission require absolute compliance. There are important exceptions and caveats in each of these contexts, but the principle we see is that there are distinct types of power granted to people, by God, based on their role.[2]

1. The language here can be misused to suggest that the earth is humanity's to treat however we want. "Subdue" and "rule" can have violent connotations, and even Christians have acted as though the creation does not really matter and we can exploit it without consequence. Human beings, however, are called to be caretakers of God's good creation. Francis Schaeffer wrote a scathing critique of Christian ecology during his day; see *Pollution and the Death of Man: The Christian View of Ecology* (Tyndale House, 1970). For a more robust Christian view of ecology, see Richard Bauckham, *The Bible and Ecology: Rediscovering the Community of Creation* (Baylor University Press, 2010).

2. Important caveats include the exception to authority that calls us to sin; we must always serve God and not man (see Acts 5). There are also limits to all human authority, and no one has the right to abuse their leadership or take full control of another's life, be they child, employee, parishioner, or spouse. God grants no one complete control and authority over another.

In fact, for people to flourish, there must be some imbalance of power. Andy Crouch makes this point with some helpful illustrations from the arena of corporate worship.[3] He notes that the worship leader, for example, has unequaled power during the service because he holds the microphone and plays the music. He can use this unique power to help the rest of the congregation participate in worship. But if he takes this power for himself and uses it for his own gain, he has the potential to lead the church astray—not just to sing badly or chaotically but to lead hearts away from God.

Likewise, there is an unequal distribution of power when the preacher stands up with a microphone and preaches for thirty or more minutes without interruption. He possesses more power than any other person in the room at that given moment.[4] Yet if he uses that power wisely and biblically, many will flourish as a result. Unequal power, Crouch says, is actually a gift of God for our good.

What is true in general is true in marriage too. Husbands and wives both have power, but it is distinct and unique to their roles. We see this spelled out most clearly in Paul's discussion of marriage in Ephesians 5. Here Paul identifies both a mutuality and a distinction that exists within the power dynamics of marriage.

3. Andy Crouch, *Playing God: Redeeming the Gift of Power* (IVP, 2013), 184–87.

4. Crouch points out that institutional power works only insofar as everyone is playing their role. If the congregation, for example, chooses not to listen to the preacher, then he will be speaking to an empty room—and will therefore have no power. "Ultimately, every member of any human institution bears some power and some responsibility for its flourishing. Our best leaders and our most admired celebrities, along with our most feared tyrants and despots, only have their unequal power as long as the image bearers in their institutions grant it to them." Crouch, 187.

> [Submit] to one another in the fear of Christ.
>
> Wives, submit to your husbands as to the Lord, because the husband is the head of the wife as Christ is the head of the church. He is the Savior of the body. Now as the church submits to Christ, so also wives are to submit to their husbands in everything. Husbands, love your wives, just as Christ loved the church and gave himself for her to make her holy, cleansing her with the washing of water by the word. He did this to present the church to himself in splendor, without spot or wrinkle or anything like that, but holy and blameless. In the same way, husbands are to love their wives as their own bodies. He who loves his wife loves himself. For no one ever hates his own flesh but provides and cares for it, just as Christ does for the church, since we are members of his body. For this reason a man will leave his father and mother and be joined to his wife, and the two will become one flesh. This mystery is profound, but I am talking about Christ and the church. To sum up, each one of you is to love his wife as himself, and the wife is to respect her husband. (Eph. 5:21–33)

This passage starts with an emphasis on mutuality, which we will discuss in more detail in a moment. For now, we must simply keep in mind that Christians are to practice mutual submission. After introducing the concept of submission as it pertains to fellow believers in general, Paul shifts his focus to the home and notes that wives are called to submit in a unique way to their husbands.

We can observe three important details about the wife's submission in this text. First, she is called to submit to her own husband. Nowhere does Scripture teach that women are called to submit to all men. Men do not possess special authority, power, or influence over women in general. This dynamic is reserved, uniquely, for wives and their own husbands.[5]

Second, we note that the wife is called to submit to her husband as to the Lord. The language here is intense. Husbands, after all, are not the Lord. They are fallible men and prone to all kinds of sin. But Paul believes that the marital union has the potential to reflect the dynamic relationship of Christ and his bride, the church. So, wives are called to submit as though they are reflecting the church's submission to the Lord.

Third and finally, we note that the text calls for wives to submit to their husbands in "everything." Paul wants to stress that this dynamic applies to all domains and all situations. The limits to this principle come only where sin enters the picture.

The exhaustiveness of this submission is, no doubt, troubling for women. Countless manipulative, sinful, and abusive men have used these verses to their advantage, leading to harmful results. We must observe that the text includes an important balance to potential abuses, one that is given directly to the husband. The text does establish that husbands are the heads of their homes, that they have a unique power in the marital relationship. Yet, when Paul directs his words to the hearts of men, he does not emphasize their unique power but emphasizes their unique responsibility.

Headship

Paul establishes in Ephesians 5 that husbands have the power of "headship" in the home. We can call this *positional power*. It's a type of power that is derived from a given position. This is an

5. Russell Moore, "Women, Stop Submitting to Men," *Russell Moore*, December 5, 2011, https://www.russellmoore.com/2011/12/05/women-stop-submitting-to-men/.

important concept that communicates a husband's leadership and responsibility to direct, care for, and protect his wife. Within Scripture, wives often perform similar tasks and have many of the same characteristics as husbands, but there remains a distinction between the two. The distinction is one of primary versus secondary responsibility.

We may compare this distinction to the role of a manager in the workforce. Our friend Justin is the director of plant operations at a hospital. It is his job to take care of the facility and oversee all facility improvements. He, of course, has a whole team who have the same responsibility but on a smaller scale. While each of them may describe their job similarly, the true responsibility rests with Justin. Likewise, a husband and wife together run a home, make decisions, plan for the future, and provide each other with safety, support, and stability. The greater weight, however, falls on the shoulders of the head of the home.

Influence

We have said, however, that wives have their own unique power within marriage. They are not the head of the home, but they possess a keen power of influence. We might speak of this as *relational power*. Some people have power by virtue of their specific role, but others have a power that is drawn from their connection to others. So, we can note how the boss in a workplace has power because of their position in the company. Yet workers who have garnered respect and admiration from fellow employees have influence and power of their own. This is the difference between positional and relational power. Multiple places in Scripture describe and commend the power of wifely influence. We certainly see the influence of Queen Esther with the Persian King Ahasuerus. The power of influence is an important power.

The apostle Peter actually commends this sort of wifely influence in a very important text for married couples. We will look again at 1 Peter 3 later in this book, but for the moment let us consider specifically verses 1–6.

> In the same way, wives, submit yourselves to your own husbands so that, even if some disobey the word, they may be won over without a word by the way their wives live when they observe your pure, reverent lives. Don't let your beauty consist of outward things like elaborate hairstyles and wearing gold jewelry or fine clothes, but rather what is inside the heart—the imperishable quality of a gentle and quiet spirit, which is of great worth in God's sight. For in the past, the holy women who put their hope in God also adorned themselves in this way, submitting to their own husbands, just as Sarah obeyed Abraham, calling him lord. You have become her children when you do what is good and do not fear any intimidation.

Here again Peter mentions the responsibility of wives to submit to their husbands, but what interests him specifically is the power of a wife's influence. In this case he mentions her conduct: purity, reverence, and a gentle and quiet spirit. These commendations should not be taken to mean that a wife has no place for using her words, for being bold, for speaking out directly, or for challenging her husband (we've already mentioned the significant example of Esther).[6] Peter sees here a tremendous amount of

6. One of the additional points we will make moving forward is that wives are called to be Christians first. All throughout the New Testament, Christians are called to rebuke, correct, and teach one another. These commands do not change merely because you are married to the Christian who needs your rebuke, correction, and instruction.

power in the influence of a godly wife, and he exhorts women to use that power.

He mentions a curious example: Sarah. Sarah is hardly the woman we would think of when it comes to a "gentle and quiet" spirit. She is hardly the woman we would think of as a submissive wife. Sarah, after all, ridiculed her husband's age when the angel of the Lord spoke to her, she laughed at God's promise, she pressured her husband into distrusting God and getting her maidservant pregnant. Peter picks, in our estimation perhaps, a very odd example.

Sarah is, however, a great example for the purposes of his point. Sarah is a woman who, while at times clearly sinful, is also direct and pointed. She speaks up and speaks out. She makes known what she thinks and what she wants, and still Scripture identifies her as a woman who respects her husband. She calls him "lord," meaning she continues to honor him in their relationship.[7] Peter commends her example as a good one, despite all that we know of Sarah's sordid story. The key for Peter, and for us, is the tremendous power of influence that wives possess.

Husbands and wives both have power within the marital dynamic. They both have the potential to use their power in sinful and selfish ways. Husbands certainly can use their headship to rule, squash, and crush their wives. That is the opposite of how Jesus calls us to use power in his kingdom (see Matt. 20:25–28). Wives, likewise, can use their power of influence to lead their

7. We do not believe this text is calling wives today to refer to their husbands as lord. This was a cultural expression of respect that does not need to be imported into the present day. Jesus himself insists that no one be called by such titles because we have a Messiah (see Matt. 23:9–11).

husbands astray, much like the wives of Solomon (see 1 Kings 11:3–4). The proper and biblical use of power, however, seeks the good and flourishing of others. Husbands and wives, then, have the potential to glorify God by using their power to serve their spouses. Such an approach to power within marriage creates a unique dynamic of mutual love and support.

MUTUALITY IN MARRIAGE

If husbands and wives have been given their own individual types of power within the marriage, what does it look like for them to use that power within their designated roles? They are called to use their God-given power and responsibilities to help each other flourish through mutual submission and mutual sacrifice.

Mutuality is experienced when the contribution and investment that each individual brings to the relationship is similar in quantity and value. Mutuality is not the same as complete equality because it leaves room for gender differences and role variations that are necessary for flourishing in a godly marriage. It allows for each spouse to exert their unique type of power. Then the two forms of power are not at risk of overtaking each other, and each can function without causing disunity. Essentially, mutuality focuses on the equality of the overall impact rather than creating an exact positional equality.

This means that even if their roles may require something different of a husband and a wife, each can still have an equal overall impact on their relationship, their family, their mission, and the world around them. To accomplish this equality of impact, each spouse must be equally invested, equally represented, and equally understood. Each person should be giving and receiving care (physically, emotionally, spiritually, and psychologically). They should be listening to and sharing concerns and ideas. Neither should seek to gain anything through coercion or manipulation. Choices are made together through joint input so that neither spouse dominates. Through mutuality, power and responsibility are shared so that each person flourishes. But this mutuality isn't just a practical solution—it is a biblical one.

Unity

An important goal of Christ-followers everywhere and through all generations is and has been unity. As a husband and wife seek to display the one-flesh nature of their marriage, and as their relationship exists within the body of Christ, their goal should be unity. First Corinthians 1:10 instructs the early church (as well as modern Christians) to let "there be no divisions among you" but to "be united with the same understanding and the same conviction." Jesus's passionate prayer for believers was for them to be one and to be brought to complete unity (see John 17:20–26). And Ephesians 4:2–3 makes it clear that unity in the Spirit doesn't just come to us because we are Christians. We have to "make every effort" to maintain it through humility, gentleness, patience, and forbearance with one another.

Unity is also achieved and maintained through outdoing one another in showing honor (see Rom. 12:10), doing nothing out of selfish ambition (see Phil. 2:3), and encouraging one another and building each other up (see 1 Thess. 5:11). All of these actions are the practical outworking of mutuality.

It is also important to note that because these passages are written to encourage followers of Christ as they seek to perfect their earthly relationships, they should definitely be applied within marriage as well. This may sound strange, but a husband and wife don't cease to be brother and sister in the family of God just because they married each other! Mutuality is an important aspect of a godly marriage because it is presented in the Bible as the means for achieving unity.

Mutuality is important for keeping a proper balance between the husband and wife, as it relates to both power and responsibility. A husband holds the power of headship, while the wife holds the power of influence. In all that they do, spouses must constantly hold the goal of mutuality in mind. This simply means that as they exert their power, they must consider the effect it has on their spouse. And as they carry out the various responsibilities of their role, they must be thinking of how they aid the other person.

When headship and submission become the sole defining roles in a marriage, mutuality is inevitably lost as the relationship is structured around a power imbalance rather than a partnership. In this dynamic, one spouse consistently holds decision-making power while the other exists in a state of deference, leading to an erosion of shared agency and reciprocal love. Over time, this imbalance can shape the entire function of the marriage, reducing the relational interplay to a hierarchy rather than a union. Instead of cultivating a bond in which both partners contribute their strengths, wisdom, and care in a complementary way, the marriage risks becoming a dynamic of control and compliance, in which the richness of mutual respect, shared leadership, and co-laboring in life is lost.

While some degree of imbalance in a marriage can contribute to its flourishing, as discussed in the previous section, this same imbalance can also become a source of harm when leveraged for personal gain. When one spouse's power is deemed more important than the other's, it creates an environment ripe for selfishness.

In such a dynamic, for example, a husband may be tempted to use his authority to prioritize his own desires, taking advantage of the resources, opportunities, and privileges at his disposal while neglecting the needs of his wife. Over time, this pattern leads to a marriage in which the husband thrives while his wife is overlooked, her voice diminished, and her well-being neglected. Likewise, a wife can use her power to manipulate her husband for personal gain, rather than seeking the interests of the whole family. Instead of a relationship marked by mutual care and shared flourishing, the imbalance becomes a means of self-serving power, leaving one partner to wither under the weight of inequity.

The problem with isolating marriage to a husband's headship and a wife's submission is that no boundaries or tethers keep the imbalance between the two from becoming too great. When it does, a husband may begin to think he has ultimate control and power over his wife. He can move toward oppression or disregard. Mutual submission keeps a husband and wife unified. When both are submitting to the other, a fence of accountability and deference protects their relationship.

Headship and submission are a part of the roles of husbands and wives, and yet those roles in isolation can lead to a lack of unity. An emphasis on overall mutuality in the relationship can bring balance to the marriage.

A Balancing Act

To show you what we mean, let's imagine a balancing scale that can be used to measure power, responsibility, and impact within a relationship. A little imbalance is okay in these areas, but for the most part a relationship will not function well if one side is considerably heavier than the other. So, even if headship and submission are very different in the way they function, they are not meant to be assigned drastically different value. The Scriptures actually teach us how to balance this dynamic in marriage.

There are two key pieces of information that people often overlook when they teach on, write about, or discuss marital roles—mutual submission and mutual sacrifice. It's not the roles themselves that are off balance; it is the omission of these additional details that ends up tipping the scale.

In Ephesians 5:22–23, Paul tells wives to submit to their husbands as to the Lord. Many scholars debate over the meaning of the Greek word translated "head" in verse 23 (does it mean source or leader?), but the word *submission* alone has a connotation of yielding yourself unto someone else. Yielding can't happen in isolation. There must be an object to which you are yielding. A wife yields her power to her husband, and he has a choice about what he does with her yielding. It is an unbalancing experience for a wife to yield her power, knowing that her husband can do something with that power. That is exactly where the balancing act needs to happen.

Mutual Submission

If we look back at verse 21, we see that all people (both men and women, husbands and wives) are told to submit to one another out of reverence for Christ. The Greek word for *submit* in this verse is actually the referent for the action of the wives in verse 22. So, even before he specifically tells wives to submit to their husbands, Paul makes it clear that there is to be mutual submission between both spouses. How does that help in our attempt to balance the marital power scale?

If this were a mathematical equation, one might think that adding submission to both sides would just cancel itself out, leaving no net effect. But this transaction actually establishes something very important that changes the whole power dynamic. While participating in the act of submitting to each other, husband and wife are to be revering Christ—or showing great regard, honor, devotion, and deference to him. Together they are equally acknowledging the authority that Christ has over them. This recognition of Christ's position tethers their individual powers to their source so that even if one spouse is tempted to run off with all the power, they are not going to get very far.

The ground beneath both spouses is also leveled when they understand that both husbands and wives are to show the same amount of honor to Christ. Even if the husband could claim a position above the wife, they are in the same position where it matters most—in relation to Jesus. Their position relative to each other does not change the fact that they are positionally equal before him. When it comes to Christ's kingdom, husbands and wives are coheirs. There are no favorites. There is no partiality, only mutuality.

Mutual Sacrifice

We find the second explanation of the balance between submission and authority in verse 25, where the husband is given his instructions. Husbands are told, "Love your wives, just as Christ loved the church." If you are a husband, you might be thinking, "That's easy enough. I already love my wife." If only it were that simple. A husband's authority requires him to love his wife as his own body (Eph. 5:28). He is to treat her with a mutuality that considers her cares, concerns, and desires not simply as equal to his but as if they actually *were* his. That leaves no room for him to use his authority as an excuse to get his way. One way to keep this in check is for a husband to regularly ask himself,

- Of the last five decisions I have made, how many resulted in me getting what I wanted?[8]

8. This is a question that our dear friend John Wemple developed in his

- How many of those decisions considered my wife in such a way that *I* sacrificed and *she* benefitted?
- Did I consider what it looks like to love my wife as my own body in each particular decision?

A husband's act of "submission," however, goes even deeper. The Bible challenges husbands to consider the ultimate sacrifice. Scripture doesn't simply tell husbands to love their wives, though that can be hard enough at times. Ephesians 5:25 says in its entirety, "Husbands, love your wives, just as Christ loved the church *and gave himself for her*." The gospel tells us that the way Christ gave himself up for his church was to die. Husbands are told to love their wives in such a way that they would be willing to die on their behalf.

Very few husbands end up facing a situation in which they must choose to physically die for their wives (though that would be a way of living out this verse). Ultimately, this passage is calling a husband to love his wife in such a way that the sacrificial death of Christ is exemplified in his thoughts, words, and deeds toward and about her.

Sacrifice should be a defining element for a Christian husband as he lives out his role within marriage. This may mean dying to the desire for a certain career path when his wife becomes ill or when she struggles with the lifestyle this career requires. This could mean dying to the life he had imagined for himself when his wife is unable to have children. It may require that he give up some of his hobbies in order to support her passions. It could be as simple as dying to "personal time" so he can spend time with his wife or so she can have time away from the kids. It could mean forgoing something he wants to buy in order to do something kind for her. Or it could be as difficult as speaking up to his family when they criticize her.

---

counseling. We are grateful to John for letting us include it here.

John 15:13 tells us that there is no greater way to demonstrate love for someone than to lay your life down for them. This is what Christ did for us, and this what husbands are called to do for their wives. Gifts and romantic gestures are all temporary, but sacrifice has a deep impact on the marital relationship—not to mention a lasting impact throughout eternity.

That last instruction is jarring. To give yourself up for your bride is a tall order. Husbands are often tempted to seek the benefits of their position of authority without also heeding the responsibility that it requires. The calling of headship is not an excuse for husbands to make choices at the expense of their wives or based on their own preferences. It also does not allow husbands to use their authority to control their wives. Genesis 3:16 tells us that husbands will "rule over" their spouses, but this is a description of the curse, not God's design. Husbands will have to guard themselves from the temptation to dominate.

While the give-and-take of mutuality is one way to make sure husbands do not overstep the bounds of their authority and headship, there is an ultimate fail-safe that should keep them from dominating, and that is the command to die unto themselves. Husbands are to love as Christ loved, which means sacrificing, not gaining. Authority used for personal gain has no place in the kingdom of God. It breeds selfishness, which then breeds entitlement, and that is the soil from which abuse grows.

To sum up what we have addressed so far: Christ has ultimate authority over the husband and wife, who are called to mutually submit to each other in recognition of that authority. A wife is uniquely called to submit to her husband, and her husband is called not only to love her but to lay down his life for her. In short, we could describe Paul's counsel to husbands and wives as follows:

Revere Christ.
Mutually submit to each other.
Wives, submit to husbands.
Husbands, die to self.

Given such a clear directive to husbands, a wife might be tempted to think that it is only her husband's job to be sacrificially loving. After all, husbands are the ones who are really called out in Ephesians 5. But if we take a look at the gospel of John, we will see that the call to sacrificial love is for all of us.

> I give you a new command: Love one another. Just as I have loved you, you are also to love one another. By this everyone will know that you are my disciples, if you love one another. (John 13:34–35)

Husbands are not the only ones who are called to love like Jesus. Christ commanded *all* of his followers to show his love to the world by loving one another in a way that says, "For the sake of love I will not only die to my desires for your benefit, but if necessary, I will completely die on your behalf." When a wife loves her husband in this way, she may have to give up some of her individuality and independence for the sake of mutuality and unity. She may have to set aside or reshape some of her plans so they can align with her husband's, creating a shared path forward. This sacrifice can mean adjusting career aspirations, personal goals, or even daily routines to foster unity and harmony in their life together. She may have to stay home for a season when she really wanted to work (or work when she really wanted to stay home) in order to accommodate the needs of her family. Rather than viewing any of these sacrifices as loss, a wife can see them as a way to cultivate a marriage that thrives on love, partnership, and the pursuit of something greater than individual desires.

Although plenty of wives fail to sacrifice for the good of their marriages, the more common pitfall that we have observed among wives is to over-sacrifice or to sacrifice with unhealthy motives. When a wife continually sacrifices without any recognition or reciprocation from her husband, she can become bitter or joyless in her service. Contentment and repentance may be part of the solution, but more is needed in order for her to pursue lasting change. Learning to properly communicate and to express her concern over the lack of mutuality can be the greatest help for the relationship and for her husband's spiritual health. A wife should not overlook her husband's sinful selfishness or neglect of the relationship in the name of sacrifice.

Sometimes a wife can take on an unhealthy martyr mindset, believing that she must carry the weight of the relationship alone. A marriage better reflects Christ and the church when there is mutual love, not one-sided exhaustion. You cannot build the health of an entire marriage on the back of one spouse, nor should you continually sacrifice in order to avoid rejection or keep the peace. Further, the wife need not be the only one to lay aside her own aspirations in order for her husband to succeed. A godly marriage involves a give-and-take. Maybe neither spouse completely fulfills all their goals and plans, but a wife's insistence on being the only one to give up anything does not make for a healthy marriage. Of course, aggressively insisting on her own way is not the answer either. Learning to humbly and graciously make requests is a vital part of a loving relationship.

Sacrifice also does not mean suppressing your opinion or putting yourself in harm's way. In order for mutuality to work, a wife should use her voice to contribute to the choices made in the relationship. It may be necessary for a wife to sacrifice some of her ideas and contributions, but she should not sacrifice her voice and agency in the process of following her husband's leadership. In the courtroom of decision-making, he may be the foreman or spokesman who represents the final choices made by the jury, but wives should not think of their husbands as the judge or the entire jury.

Most importantly, enduring mistreatment from one's spouse is not a form of Christlike sacrifice. When Christians are called to "turn the other cheek" in Jesus's Sermon on the Mount, we are not being asked to sacrifice our safety and dignity but to end any cycle of revenge and retaliation (see Matt. 5:39). This same Jesus encourages us to flee persecution whenever possible (see Matt. 10:23). We are most definitely not commanded to dismiss sinful behavior in marriage. Loving, mutual sacrifice does not mean enabling abuse, control, or manipulation.

In light of these important guidelines, it may be helpful for a wife to evaluate her sacrifice with the following questions:

- Have the sacrifices I made for my husband and family this week led me to be resentful, or have I made them in genuine love and a desire for unity?
- Is there something I need to talk to my husband about that could restore the balance of mutuality? Am I resistant to addressing that issue? If so, why?
- Are there any life goals that I sat aside at one time but would like to revisit? Are there any plans I have been selfishly holding on to that I might need to sacrifice for the sake of my marriage?
- Do I know how to graciously and effectively make requests of my husband?

A frustration we have had in parenting our three children is their constant focus on personal gain. They fight over the best seat in the car. They argue over who will get the biggest piece of dessert. They game the system so that the other sibling has to do the worst chores. In trying to teach them the important lesson of self-sacrifice, we find ourselves constantly repeating the same refrain: "Everything would go so much smoother for all of you if you would focus on giving rather than taking. If you all commit to sacrifice for one another, then you will still end up getting something you want, and your relationship won't be so difficult. Isn't it really tiring to fight for the biggest and best and most desirable all the time?"

A good relationship may not be the most enticing reward for teenage siblings, but it should be for a godly couple. As Tim Keller writes in his book *The Meaning of Marriage*, biblical teaching on marriage "does not offer a choice between fulfillment and sacrifice but rather mutual fulfillment through mutual sacrifice."[9] Practically speaking, outdoing each other through sacrifice accomplishes far more than selfishness ever could. Not only will you continue to do and have things that are important to you as your spouse sacrifices for your sake, but you will also build trust and relational capital with them as you do the same. Mutuality builds a stronger and more enjoyable marital relationship.

A WARNING TO EXHORT

Of course, mutuality isn't always equally pursued by both spouses. Although it is undeniably frustrating and difficult, a

9. Timothy Keller, *The Meaning of Marriage: Facing the Complexities of Commitment with the Wisdom of God*, with Kathy Keller (Dutton, 2011), 43.

lack of mutuality—which leads to a lack of the positive feedback loop mentioned above—does not give you permission to stop sacrificing. Just as we don't stop doing good to others because they aren't doing good to us (see Matt. 7:12), we don't stop sacrificing for our spouses when they aren't sacrificing for us. And we can even fulfill our role as spouses with a respectful and loving heart. Without the mutuality of sacrifice, it is hard to have a marriage that is healthy and satisfying, but God can nonetheless empower you to live well amid this challenging situation.

Within all our relationships, including marriage, we are called to speak the truth in love. This is all the more important when a spouse's selfish choices are affecting innocent children and an entire family structure. If your spouse is self-centered and arrogant, it is not only unnecessary but also unwise to allow them to continue. It isn't selfish to speak up when your spouse wrongs you. In fact, the negative impact on you—and your willingness to address it—may be the only warning sign that alerts them to their waywardness.[10]

Hebrews 3:13 (ESV) tells us to "exhort one another every day" so that no one will be "hardened by the deceitfulness of sin." When we don't speak up about the misuse of power in our marriage relationships, we are giving an opportunity for our spouses' hearts to be hardened by the deceitfulness of sin. Sacrifice means doing what is best for the other person even when it is difficult, and sometimes that involves confrontation.

10. If you are in an abusive relationship, confrontation will necessarily be very different. It is not wise to confront an abuser without proper help and protection. It is important for you first to evaluate if your relationship is abusive and then to seek the proper help before moving forward with any kind of confrontation.

MUTUALITY WITH DISTINCTIONS

The Bible's message of mutuality conflicts with much of what we hear taught today. Mutuality considers the way our actions and decisions affect our spouses. It also understands that in God's eyes neither gender is more privileged, and therefore our differing roles are not to be considered more or less valuable. In this sense, mutuality contrasts not only with what the world considers to be true but also with the way in which many Christian marriages operate.

First Corinthians 11 can be a tough passage to interpret, but it holds an important message about mutuality. Paul writes to the Corinthians to address certain issues that were causing problems within the church. Some people were enjoying their liberties a little too much, and some were unwilling to let go of unnecessary laws so that they could embrace the freedom of the new covenant. Things got very confusing. There were a lot of questions regarding what to get rid of and what to hold on to, what was fulfilled in Christ and what is still required for displaying Christ to the world. Because the passage is so heavily drenched in cultural context, it is hard to tell what is a principle for us to follow now and what is simply tied to the context of the early church.

Essentially, Paul's goal is to correct certain behaviors within the church so that the gospel message will not be tainted in the eyes of the watching world. In this particular chapter, Paul has been told that the men and women are not honoring each other—specifically as it pertains to head coverings. As a result of this, they are failing to properly distinguish themselves as male and female.

People often use this text to argue that the proper position of women is to be subordinate to men, that the proper position of men is to be in authority over women, and that these positions are essential because God designed them that way. But if you read to the end of this passage, the way Paul wraps up his instruction communicates a message of mutuality that is frequently overlooked. He concludes by explaining that neither man nor woman exists without the other, so neither man nor woman has priority over the other.

> In the Lord, however, woman is not independent of man, and man is not independent of woman. For just as woman came from man, so man comes through woman, and all things come from God. (1 Cor. 11:11–12)

Paul's claim is that gender does not determine priority in a godly relationship. He is undermining any and all gender-based abuses of power within the body of Christ while maintaining and uplifting the differences that God has created between men and women. This explains our desire for mutuality within Christian marriages. We do not desire for gender to be blurred or even for the specific roles to blend into each other. Paul maintains those gender differences throughout chapter 11. What we should long for is that Christians would maintain and even celebrate their differences while also using those differences to support one another.

Our roles are meant to complement each other. God intended that we use our differences to help one another flourish. This means we are to mutually fill in where the other lacks. We each equally need the other, and we each equally need to give of ourselves.

PRACTICING MUTUALITY

A couple has numerous decisions to make and patterns to establish as they build a home together. Each of these decisions and patterns creates the potential for power struggles to unravel the closely woven strands of a family. But there is also the potential for a husband and wife to combine their power and responsibility to achieve the family's overall goals. The give-and-take of mutuality is vital for planning who will perform certain tasks within the home. Understanding what goals they want to achieve can help a couple discern what direction they ought to go and how they can get there.

When you start assigning jobs for an undecided, ambiguous purpose, your work can feel pointless. Doing things, for example, simply because that's how they were done in your family of origin may not be what is best for your family now that you are married. It is also important to understand what the Bible says (and doesn't say) about certain responsibilities that have traditionally been regarded a man's or woman's duty. Often the principles for such responsibilities are derived from misunderstandings and misapplications of Scripture. Untangling principles from tradition is an arduous task, but doing so can release a couple from the legalism that often trips up even the most scripturally committed family.

For example, the Bible doesn't state that husbands take out the trash and cut the grass or that wives cook the food and clean the house.[11] Dividing responsibilities this way may work well for many families, but that is because it fits with the culture we live in and not necessarily because this system comes directly from Scripture. Various countries around the world have their own ways of dividing tasks, since their workforce operates differently and their history as it pertains to work is not the same as ours. But Christians in such contexts do not have to upend the whole system. They can live very naturally in a setting like this, and

11. See Winston T. Smith, *Who Does the Dishes? Decision Making in Marriage* (New Growth Press, 2008).

they can still show Christ to others through their commitment to sacrifice, their devotion to mutual submission, and their focus on honoring others and valuing the opposite gender.

It is perfectly fine for your family to implement a traditional division of labor, as long as that choice is made for the right reason. When carried out with mutual respect—without control or force from the husband and without disdain or resentment from the wife—assigning work outside the home to the husband and work inside the home to the wife can align with biblical teaching. But, like everything that is done for the wrong reasons, this way of dividing tasks can become distorted and legalistic. It is possible to stick to the principles of Scripture and have a husband who works at home and does the cooking and cleaning and a wife who works a job outside the home and does the yard work and car maintenance. When the biblical standard is understood and applied properly, husbands and wives have many different ways to assign tasks within the home while still pleasing God.

Titus 2:5 is one verse that is often treated as a broad command for wives, but the larger principle derived from the text helps us interpret it more carefully. In context, Paul is listing qualities that older women need to teach younger women. Contained within this list is the idea that young wives should be "workers at home." Many Christians have assumed this to mean that wives shouldn't work outside the home, but that application fails to grasp the actual principle contained in the text.

Looking closely at the biblical and cultural context for Titus 2:5, we see that Paul was sorting out confusion and opposing false teaching by explaining how Christian values should be applied in ancient Crete. He seeks not only to protect Christians from false teachers but also to preserve the purity of the gospel and teach believers how to live out this truth before the world.

One of Paul's specific concerns was that women of the early church were being led astray by false teachers. One commonly held interpretation is that the women were being encouraged "to rebel openly against their husbands . . . and to dress seductively as an expression of that rebellion."[12] Elsewhere, Paul further explains that wolves were creeping "into households" and capturing "gullible women overwhelmed by sins" (2 Tim. 3:6). These women were being "led astray by a variety of passions, always learning and never able to come to a knowledge of the truth" (v. 7).[13]

Paul is not limiting wives to working at home (that wouldn't make sense, given that on other occasions he actually encouraged the women who were working outside the home to aid his ministry). In fact, he simply wanted to protect them from the false teachers who were drawing them away. "Working at home" is contrasted with the behavior of some young women who were going around their neighborhoods gossiping and being lazy rather than managing their homes well. So, it wasn't necessarily about the location of their work but the fact that they were neglecting it. It would have been possible for them to tend to their families in very productive way without always being at home.[14]

12. William D. Mounce, *Pastoral Epistles*, Word Biblical Commentary 46 (repr., Zondervan, 2000), lxxiv.

13. This description is not being applied to the female gender in general but is simply expressing the state of these particular women. Women of various eras, including this one, have been intentionally deprived of education and rarely instructed in the skills needed for discernment. This put them in a position where they might easily be led astray. It would make sense, then, why Paul would want women (at younger ages and early on in his ministry) to stay protected, while he later entrusted them (at older ages and later in his ministry) to take on more responsibility.

14. We see this in the example of the Proverbs 31 wife, who buys and sells at the market.

But, as is the case with any sin we are likely to commit, it is best to remove the temptation when a sin is crouching and ready to pounce. Paul wanted the young women to stay focused, avoid their own sinful desires and temptations, and learn to value the work that they had agreed to do—all of which would help their families to flourish. *That* is the principle we can apply in our cultural context.

When a husband and wife create a thriving system of mutuality within their home, the individual and collective flourishing that they enjoy will spill out into the world around them. As they build into each other's lives through submission and sacrifice, everyone in the family can benefit and grow from what they learn and receive from the other members. They impact the world as they discover how to use their own unique talents, skills, abilities, and desires, not for themselves but for the benefit of those around them. Each member can go out into the world with a flourishing presence.

A flourishing family makes a difference. Perhaps a family business can be a beacon of honesty, commitment, and dependability within the community. Or maybe family meals can be stretched to share with neighbors. The training a child receives within their home can help them speak the gospel into the lives of their classmates. A family's musical skills can allow them to reach others for Christ or spread joy to their church and the wider community. Creating an atmosphere of learning, reading, and exploring can inspire family members to be more curious about God's amazing creation, which can lead them to share their discoveries with the people in their circles of influence. The daily example of parents reading and applying Scripture fosters an environment in which each family member receives a solid foundation for their own flourishing, one that will carry over into their future family. If the members of a household take time to plan well together, internalizing proper biblical values ahead of time, their influence can travel far beyond their home.

Priscilla and Aquila model that ripple effect of a flourishing family. The life they lived together displayed mutual submission, sacrifice, consideration, and unity, and the benefits they experienced in their marriage extend out into the church to this day. They exemplified mutual submission by working together in their trade and ministry without a strict hierarchy between them. In Acts 18:26, they both take Apollos aside to teach him about the faith more accurately, showing that they valued each other's wisdom and worked as a team in discipling others. The fact that Priscilla's name is sometimes mentioned first (see Rom. 16:3; 2 Tim. 4:19) suggests that she played a significant role and that Aquila did not seek to dominate or silence her. Instead, they modeled a relationship in which both voices mattered and in which they submitted to each other's strengths for the sake of their shared mission in Christ.

The couple's sacrifices were evident in their willingness to uproot their lives multiple times to serve the early church. They had to leave Rome due to persecution (see Acts 18:2) and later risked their lives for Paul (see Rom. 16:3–4), showing that their marriage was not about personal gain or self-preservation but about serving God and others together. Neither partner clung to personal comfort; instead, they sacrificed stability and safety to fulfill their shared calling. Their home also became a meeting place for the church (see 1 Cor. 16:19), demonstrating their shared willingness to use their resources and personal space for the benefit of others.

Every major move Priscilla and Aquila made—whether relocating, opening their home, or ministering to others—was made in unity, as we can see by the way they are never mentioned separately in Scripture but always together. Their unity allowed them to serve effectively because they were aligned in priority and purpose. Whether in their trade, ministry, or personal sacrifices, they were always working together, presenting a picture of a marriage rooted in oneness rather than individual pursuits. Their unity wasn't about losing individuality but about embracing a shared calling.

Because Priscilla and Aquila walked in step with each other, they were able to provide a stable and powerful presence in the early church, strengthening others through their partnership and living as an example to all Christian couples at all points in history. When spouses consider each other, sacrifice for the good of the other, and submit to one another, their marriage becomes a reflection of Christ's love and mutual service. Marriages built on unity, shared purpose, and selfless love can be powerful witnesses within families, churches, communities, and world.

Though the work of Priscilla and Aquila culminated in formal ministry through going on missions and forming a house church, mutuality can bring flourishing even if your marriage does not lead to formal ministry of any kind. Flourishing should not be determined by our earthly ideas of grandeur. The gospel can be taken into the world even if you aren't missionaries or church planters. In fact, mutuality may mean that you sacrifice a desire for formal ministry because it shows the greatest love for your spouse or your entire family. God does not bless pastors and ministry leaders if such work is pursued at the expense of others' needs and well-being. Mutuality takes a great amount of faith. But you can know that God will work for your good even when you must give up what you imagined would be the good he was doing.

QUESTIONS FOR REFLECTION

1. This chapter emphasized mutuality. In what ways have you experienced mutuality even within a power imbalance (perhaps at work or church)? How has that been good?
2. Ephesians 5 explores marriage roles not in terms of privileges but in terms of mutual sacrifice. How does reading the text this way impact your understanding of marital roles?
3. What influenced the way you and your spouse approach managing the home? What might need to change about how you manage your home to better meet the needs of your household?
4. How can the flourishing of your home be a blessing to the world?

3 A SHARED FAMILY VISION

Why are there so many "power struggles" within marriages? We can answer this question simplistically and say, "Because of sin!" We might even identify the root of the issue as selfishness. Both answers are true, of course, but they don't offer us a clear way forward. So let's get more specific: At the heart of a power struggle between husband and wife is a lack of shared vision.

Many marital power struggles have at their core not merely a battle of wills but a fundamental misalignment of purpose. When two people enter into marriage without a shared vision, they may find themselves working against each other rather than alongside each other. Decisions about careers, parenting, finances, and even leisure can become battlegrounds rather than opportunities to collaborate. A lack of unity in purpose inevitably leads them to compete for control, as each spouse feels the need to assert their way rather than seek a way forward together. But when a couple develops a shared vision for their marriage—one that aligns with God's design for mutual flourishing—they move from opposition to partnership, from power struggles to shared strength.

This is where mutuality becomes essential. Rather than seeing power as something to be grasped or wielded against one another, husbands and wives can use their strengths for the good of the whole. When both spouses commit to a vision in which each person's voice is valued and their gifts are used to serve each other, the marriage begins to thrive.

This kind of partnership doesn't happen by accident—it requires intentionality, grace, and a willingness to surrender personal agendas for the sake of something greater. But no matter how long a couple has struggled to work together, God's redemptive power can reshape their marriage, bringing new depth, purpose, and joy to their shared life.

We have talked about mutuality as a way for husbands and wives to use their power to help each other flourish. As their family begins to take shape, mutuality and power can also be used to help the entire household flourish. It is ideal to start planning for a life of mutuality as early as possible so that you can set a precedent for future interactions. But it is never too late to start considering how mutuality could change the dynamic that already exists within your family. God can redeem lost time that is surrendered to him. Even if you have lived twenty, thirty, forty, or fifty years in a marriage full of gridlock and frustration, our God can restore your relationship and redeem the pursuits of your family.

Creating a shared vision that properly represents each member of the home means considering what the husband and wife understand about marital roles and how that applies to various areas of managing a home. These areas may comprise the character, spirituality, health, and education of each member of the family. They can also include chores, traditions, hospitality, maintenance, repairs, finances, values, goals, and much more. It may be helpful to consider what both spouses experienced in their own families of origin, what they want to hold on to from this history, what they want to let go of, what is personally important to them, and what they are willing to give up for the sake of the plans that they make together. Here are a few questions to consider:

- Does each person want to live near family?
- What kind of compromises is each person willing to make when it comes to relocating?
- What are each person's goals, and how do they fit together?
- What are each person's strengths, and how do they fit together?
- What are each person's weaknesses, and how might they conflict?
- How do these combined strengths and weaknesses balance one another?
- What is each person good at?
- What is each person able to do?
- What things need to be accomplished that neither person is good at or likes to do?
- What can each person learn to do for the sake of the family?

It's impossible to foresee every issue that may come up, but if you take time to consider what mutuality might look like in your household, you may be able to avoid some major conflicts regarding power dynamics, roles, and responsibilities. Or if your marriage is well underway, you can walk step-by-step through these questions and make any necessary changes to the existing structure of the home. Prioritizing ongoing reflection and intentional effort will help build a marriage that grows in balance, understanding, and mutual care over time.

WHAT IS A SHARED FAMILY VISION?

Everyone comes into marriage with their own story, their own goals and agenda, their own interests and aspirations. But the "one-flesh union" of marriage is about creating something new. When you get married, you aren't simply adding someone else to your story; you are writing a new story together. You aren't merely attaching someone to your preexisting life; you are making a new life together. A husband comes into marriage as blue water, and a wife comes into marriage as red water, but together they are to become purple water.[1] A marriage that does not mix properly will look like blue or red water, meaning one spouse will not be represented in the shared life. Couples must purpose to create a vision for their lives that genuinely represents both of them: a shared family vision.

Many people have crafted vision statements for their personal lives, companies, ministries, or churches, but very few people write one for their families. Vision statements define what an organization stands for and what its future is oriented toward accomplishing. Similarly, a family vision seeks to establish its values and goals, to prioritize what is most important to that specific family unit. A shared family vision seeks to honor the personalities, histories, and values of each spouse and create something that includes both husband and wife. As such, it should feel mutually inclusive. It should be the result of conversation, compromise, and prayer. It should present a vision of the future that you can both be excited about and motivated to pursue together. It should feel unifying and honoring.

1. We are indebted to our colleague and friend Denise Hardy, who shared this illustration with us.

HOW DOES A SHARED FAMILY VISION HELP COUPLES RESOLVE POWER STRUGGLES?

A shared family vision establishes the joint priorities of a household. Often couples get into power struggles because they have conflicting agendas that are rooted in competing visions for life. By contrast, an agreed-on vision for life provides them a means by which to evaluate their ideas, goals, and activities. It allows a couple to assess whether something fits with what they have together deemed to be their priorities as a family. For example, if a couple prioritizes being active in their local church, and if moving to the country would significantly hinder that, their shared family vision helps guide their decision on whether to stay put or move. Power struggles can be dramatically mitigated if you cultivate shared priorities and values through a vision statement.

A document like this doesn't, of course, resolve all disagreements, but it does help moderate the power struggles that can arise out of conflict. It provides an agreed-on means of evaluating decisions and priorities, which then guides couples as they work through challenges. In this regard, a shared family vision focuses their individual uses of power. Spiritual leadership and spiritual guidance can be directed toward specific shared goals rather than wielded in competition with each other. Husbands can lead their families toward a shared vision of life. Wives can influence decisions toward that same shared vision.

Furthermore, a shared vision removes the persistent need for husbands to play the "tiebreaker" card. There is a common belief among many Christians that when a husband and wife disagree about something, the husband has "final say." He is the ultimate tiebreaking "decider." Now, we affirm the husband's spiritual leadership in the home and believe that there are cases where he must exercise that kind of decision-making authority—but how this is done is exceedingly important.

Sometimes men use this concept of "final say" as a way of simply getting what they want. A man deems his vision for the future as what is "best for the family," and so he makes the final decision and encourages his wife to trust him and submit to his decision. There are times when this may have to happen in a marriage, but we believe such situations should be extremely rare and supported by a wife's trust that her husband values her perspective and genuinely believes that his is the best option. A husband who frequently plays the "tiebreaker" card to get his own way will violate his wife's trust, and she will begin to feel undervalued and underrepresented in their marriage. A shared family vision makes this type of leadership move less necessary.

If a couple regularly faces unresolvable conflicts and simply cannot come to agreement, it usually means that they have different visions for life. Drafting a shared family vision can help them better navigate disagreement and cut down on the number of disagreements that they have. It won't resolve all your conflicts, but it will certainly help.

HOW DO WE CRAFT A SHARED FAMILY VISION?

In what follows we will outline a process for crafting your own family vision. For convenience, and to facilitate conversation, we have broken down the process into four phases.[2]

2. A wonderful resource for further study on crafting a family vision is Mark Scandrette and Lisa Scandrette, *Belonging and Becoming: Creating a Thriving Family Culture* (IVP, 2016).

Phase One: Gather Data

The first thing you'll need to do in shaping a family vision is gather data about your own values and priorities, as well as those of your spouse. Answer these questions and ask your spouse to do the same.

- How do you determine what is most important to you?
- What were the core values of your family of origin?
- Which values from your family of origin do you want to maintain, and which do you want to let go?
- How do you want to cultivate meaningful relationship with each other?
- How do others (extended family, friends, church members, neighbors, and so on) fit into our world?
- Are there any gifts, strengths, interests, or passions that are unique to our family? Is there anything we do as a family that we can use to serve others?
- What are the nonnegotiables for our lives? What do we value most as a family? Does our lifestyle match our stated values and nonnegotiables?
- How important is church to our family?
- What are our long-term goals for our family as a whole, for our marriage, and for each of our kids? (These may all be different.)
- What Scriptures inform us on the purpose of our lives?

Phase Two: Discuss

As you and your spouse, and perhaps your children, answer these questions, it will be valuable for you to discuss your answers with one another. Your answers will probably have significant differences. That should be expected because you are all different people with different histories and experiences. In discussion you want to identify both common ground and disagreement. Consider the following questions together.

- What are some of the commonalities between our answers to the above questions? Is there anything that we all agree on or come close to agreeing on? Record any common areas of agreement.
- Where do we disagree? What are the reasons for our answers? (Discuss without judging one another's answers.) How have our personal experiences shaped our answers?
- What is the nature of our disagreement? Is it philosophical (that is, we approach life differently), methodological (that is, we want the same thing, but we disagree on how to achieve that goal), or personal (that is, a matter of personal preference)?
- In the areas in which we disagree, what can I appreciate about the other person's perspective? Why do I appreciate that?

Phase Three: Draft a Vision

We are now in a position to put together a first draft of our family vision. Based on the information you have gathered, what stands out as the most important values of your family? Start with the answers that reflect the most common ground and then discuss how to craft a vision that embraces everyone's perspective. Make compromises and work to embrace everyone's interests and desires.

The key to crafting a good vision is to make it concise, memorable, and focused. Your family vision should have three to five core values, and you should be able to express them simply. Consider the following example.

Deb and Zac found that they had a lot of agreement in the area of church. Church was really important to them, and they knew that whatever vision they crafted as a family, church involvement would be a central focus. They did not, however, agree on spending time with extended family. Zac felt a burden to care for his parents, but Deb never had a close relationship with her mom (her dad had left when she was very young), and so she felt like Zac was putting too much emphasis on extended family. The more they talked, however, the more they were able to understand each other's perspective and come to some agreement. While extended family needed to be a part of their shared vision, they would have a twice-yearly checkup that allowed Deb to voice concern if she felt that extended family were taking up too much time. So, their formal vision statement read,

> We are committed to loving and serving God's family, our family, and extended family.

The order of those words was intentionally agreed on. The vision provided a built-in priority scale, as well as a means of evaluating decisions. When a family event was going to require missing too much church, then their vision statement told them it wasn't a good idea. When working on Grandpa's house meant missing another one of Johnny's karate tournaments, then Zac rescheduled with his dad. The vision offered a framework for evaluating what they did each week and helped hold them both accountable to their stated priorities.

Consider a couple of other sample family vision statements:

Kevin and Stacey

- *Help.* We are both biblical counselors in our church, and we want to keep serving there.
- *Hospitality.* We believe in loving our friends and neighbors by having them in our home.
- *Holiness.* We believe it is important for us to be part of a growing and healthy church.

The Thompsons

- *Character over achievement.* Who you are matters more than what you do.
- *Respect over resolution.* How we speak to one another is more important than resolving our conflicts.
- *Responsibilities before pleasure.* We do our work before we play.
- *Community before technology.* We spend more time face-to-face than face-to-device.
- *God over others.* God is the most important person in our lives, and we live to honor him.

Draft a vision with your family that highlights your collective core values. Remember, this is not *your* vision but your shared vision; it should represent everyone involved.

Phase Four: Evaluate

Once you have agreed on your vision, take a few months to practice living according to it and then schedule a time to evaluate yourselves. Sometimes we need to make adjustments, either to our vision (it doesn't fit us, it isn't realistic, and so on) or to our lifestyle (we like our vision, but we need to change the way we live in order to abide by it). Plan a date for reevaluation and put it on your calendar. Do this again every so often to keep the vision fresh. As you and your family change, you may need to realign with your values, or you may find that part of your vision needs to change.

CONCLUSION

In a broken and fallen world, we know that we will have problems, and we know that we will encounter power struggles. There is no way to completely avoid this reality. Yet godly couples can navigate these power struggles by reminding themselves of the purpose of power: God has given each of us a type of power so that we can help others flourish.

If you are a husband, you have been given the role of spiritual leader in your home. But that is a role that uses power under instead of power over. This use of power reflects that of our Lord and Savior, who came not to be served but to serve.

If you are a wife, you have been given the role of spiritual helper. You have a type of power that can influence your husband. You can dramatically shape the culture of your home through your power; use it to reflect the love of Christ to the members of your household.

Together, husbands and wives can create not just a shared vision of a good life but the reality of a shared life that blesses everyone in the home and spills out into the world. As a family, you can use power in your home to point to the glorious gospel of grace, in which our all-powerful God sacrificed himself in order to bring us into spiritual life. May your home be a living picture of this amazing truth.

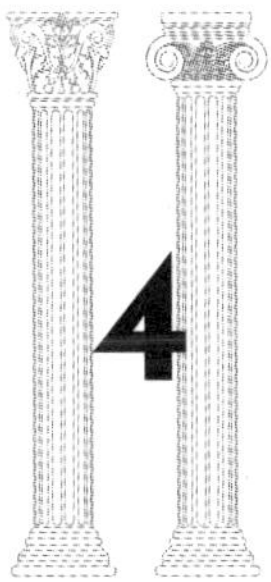

4

A HUSBAND'S USE OF POWER

What does it actually look like to be the "spiritual leader" in your home? This is not a small question. Get it wrong, and it can lead to devastation, heartache, and harm. Get it right, and it can lead to flourishing, blessing, and beauty.

Jim was the master of his domain. He led his family with a strong hand and felt it was his right—indeed, his duty—to make decisions for his wife. He did this without a thought toward her needs, personality, interests, or capabilities. He was in charge. Cal, on the other hand, was passive and disengaged from anything having to do with the family. He worked hard, earned money, and then enjoyed his personal hobbies. His wife made all the major decisions regarding the household, the future, and their personal plans. He was along for the ride.

Both of these men had fundamentally missed their calling as husbands. According to Scripture, power and leadership are given for the sake of serving others. Spiritual leadership in the home, then, exercises power under (as opposed to power over) another person. It is power used to lift others up. In particular, it is power that provides three things: safety, support, and stability for the other members of the family.

UNIQUE POWER

It's important to note at the outset of this chapter that a husband's power is unique. While it's true that wives also have power, each has a distinct type of power. As heads, husbands are called to lead, meaning they have a greater responsibility to take initiative and prioritize the direction and care of the family. Throughout Scripture, when the sin of Adam and Eve is mentioned, it is often described specifically as Adam's sin. He is the one who stands as the representative of this failure (see Hos. 6:7; Rom. 5:14; 1 Cor. 15:22). To be a spiritual leader is to bear the greater weight of responsibility.

Wives also bear responsibility, of course, and they also help to lead and direct a home. But they have different degrees of responsibility and leadership. In fact, while we focus on safety, support, and stability, we can readily recognize ways in which wives provide these things as well. Yet husbands are to take the lead in these areas, and so they will bear greater responsibility for them. The husband's role is unique, even if it overlaps with his wife's.

THE CORE ELEMENTS OF HEADSHIP

The following categories are not the only way you can break down the responsibilities of a husband. They do, however, capture several key elements of his unique position and power. So, let's unpack each of these elements in some detail in order to better understand a husband's role.

Safety

Safety can seem like a straightforward category. It is a husband's job to protect his family. But often we think exclusively in terms of physical protection. That is a legitimate issue and one in which husbands should take the lead. Yet we must also consider other forms of safety, such as financial, spiritual, and emotional safety. Emotional safety is of particular importance, and it often gets overlooked in discussions of marital dynamics. A husband should be the safest person in the world for his wife. She should sense that she can share with him anything and he will respect her emotions, listen fully, and care about what is important to her. Peter urges husbands to "live with [their] wives in an understanding way" (1 Peter 3:7). A husband should be attuned to his wife's needs, fears, desires, and insecurities. He should know her personality and temptations, her strengths and weaknesses. He should be sensitive to her. Peter warns that the husband who doesn't live this way will find that God does not hear his prayers. The Lord takes emotional safety in the home quite seriously. Husband, are you a safe person for your wife?

Likewise, husbands should be concerned with financial safety. The Scriptures expect that husbands and fathers will do all that they reasonably can to provide for the family's material needs (see 1 Tim. 5:8). Of course, no one can control the economy, and there may come seasons throughout your life when finances are tighter. Companies have to lay off workers, and job searches can take substantial time. Overall, however, as a husband, you must seek to provide financial safety for your family. This may include planning for the future, saving for retirement, and preparing for emergencies. It may mean getting life insurance. Those are all challenging issues that each family will need to weigh based on what they can afford. More fundamentally, husbands will want to initiate regular conversations and evaluations in which the family can assess whether they are living within their means. Husband, have you created financial safety for your family?

Finally, we should mention physical safety. Husbands need to do all that they can to ensure their families' physical safety. Does the family have a safe home with a roof overhead? Does the family have access to the medical care they may need? Many years ago, we helped a family whose front door did not open. This was a major safety concern, and I challenged the husband to take responsibility for getting it fixed. He was not protecting his family. Husband, have you created safety in your home?

Ask your wife about her sense of safety. Does she feel safe? Listen without getting defensive, and be prepared to pursue changes if she offers some areas of concern. Perhaps there are some immediate changes you can make to your home or finances. You can also consult with a financial planner if needed. Or maybe you need to address some issues in your character, so contacting a biblical counselor would be an important next step for you. Whatever the specific needs may be, you can and should make changes to promote safety in your home.

Support

Next, consider support. To support someone means to aid their success. It involves our emotional sensitivity and physical care. We return again to the idea of living with your spouse in an "understanding way." Being understanding requires compassion, empathy, and care. Paul encourages all Christians to maintain an interest in the desires and concerns of others.

> If, then, there is any encouragement in Christ, if any consolation of love, if any fellowship with the Spirit, if any affection

> and mercy, make my joy complete by thinking the same way, having the same love, united in spirit, intent on one purpose. Do nothing out of selfish ambition or conceit, but in humility consider others as more important than yourselves. Everyone should look not to his own interests, but rather to the interests of others. (Phil. 2:1–4)

The alternative to living with selfish ambition and conceit, says Paul, is to regard others as more important than yourself. One tangible way to do that is to prioritize their interests alongside your own. So, to support your wife means, in part, to take an interest in what interests her.

I (Dave) support my wife, for example, when I listen to her heart and care about its burdens and joys. When she is sad, I listen and give her space to share all her emotions with me. When she is afraid, I comfort her. When she is excited about a project, I listen with enthusiasm and find ways to encourage her in such endeavors. Support begins with emotional sensitivity. I pay attention to how she feels, and I seek to match her emotional energy in an appropriate way. But support is more than just emotional sensitivity; it is also accompanied by action and physical care. I take some kind of action to demonstrate my support. I move to help her and see her thrive.

Several years ago, Krista aspired to do more writing. She's a great writer and has tremendous creativity. She also lacks confidence at times; but, because this work was important to her, I knew that I needed to find a way to help her pursue it. I wanted to see her thrive in this area, and so I encouraged her and took action to help her. I dragged an old vintage desk out of the basement and cleaned it up. I moved it to our den and rearranged the furniture so that the desk was in front of a big open window. I set her up with a lovely little workspace and bought her some new writing tools. These were simple gestures, and in the grand scheme of things, they didn't amount to much in terms of helping her actually write. But they demonstrated my support and my desire to see her accomplish something that I believed she was good at.[1] Husband, does your wife feel supported by you?

If you can't answer that question positively, know that you can grow in your support. Start by seeking to understand your wife better. Ask her about her longings, fears, joys, and dreams. Identify small tangible ways you can encourage her in any of those areas. Seek to take an interest in something that interests her. It may be difficult for you at first, perhaps even a bit frustrating, but you can cultivate this kind of care as you practice giving support.

Stability

Finally, we should consider stability. We often think of stability in terms of having a firm place to put our feet. It is the psychological and emotional sense that our life has a level of predictability. This predictability generally allows us to live with peace and freedom in the home. Husbands have a tremendous opportunity to give their wives a firm footing by their consistency.

To thrive, a wife needs to know what to expect from her husband and from the culture of their home. This means he must be a person of integrity whom his wife can rely on. She needs to see consistency in his character. She needs to trust that he will be a man of God even when it's not convenient. She should expect her husband to show grace, to hold to what is true, and to bear the fruit of the Spirit. No man is perfect, of course, but there should

1. Admittedly, I wish I were this thoughtful more often. I still have lots of room to grow in the principles I commend.

be a general predictability in his character. If a wife never knows which version of her husband she will get on any given day, she will live with constant fear and frustration.

Likewise, there should be predictability in the culture of the home. Do the goals and values of your home change constantly? Does a husband regularly change careers, churches, friendships? This kind of instability makes it hard for wives to know their roles and responsibilities and to pursue their own interests. Stability, then, is a vital gift a husband can give to his spouse.

Navigating instability is like trying to cross a rickety rope bridge with missing slats. With every step, the planks creak, the ropes sway, and doubt takes hold. Will the bridge support our weight? Will we slip through the gaps? A husband who creates an atmosphere of instability hinders connection and reliability. Every conversation feels risky to his wife, and she moves cautiously and slowly.

Stability, in contrast, is like walking across a solid, well-built bridge. Most people feel confident and secure in such a situation. Each step is supported by a strong foundation, allowing them to move forward without hesitation. They don't have to question whether the next step will hold them—they walk across without even thinking about it. A husband who displays this kind of stability will bring unity and trust to the marriage. His wife will see him as reliable and consistent.

Husband, have you created stability in your home? Evaluate your own heart and life. Humbly seek out and listen to the feedback your wife may have. If she doesn't feel like there is stability in her world due to flaws in your character, seek out help to address those issues. If there are tasks that need to be finished because you have repeatedly procrastinated finishing them, do whatever you have to do to get the job done. Make a plan, gather resources, ask for help, form a team—take action and stop only for reasonable breaks. Where you have made commitments, follow up on them as soon as possible (and continue to consistently do so). With effort and support, you can reduce any instability you may have created and provide a steadier foundation for your wife to rest on.

BUT WHAT ABOUT DECISION-MAKING?

If you are at all familiar with the conversation surrounding biblical manhood, then you will have spotted a notable absence in this discussion of power under: There is no mention of decision-making as a key component of a husband's role in the home. Often a husband's authority is framed almost entirely in terms of making decisions for the family, or having the "final say." That model of headship tends toward power over instead of power under (that is, top-down authority rather than power used to build up). The Bible, however, does not teach us that decision-making is the husband's job. But as a husband seeks to provide safety, support, and stability for his household, there will be rare occasions when he may ask his wife to trust him and agree to a decision that she does not fully support. There are several important elements of the decision-making process that are worth parsing out more fully.

First, decision-making is not unilaterally a husband's job. In general, husbands and wives should make decisions together. Both are called to manage the home (see 1 Tim. 3:4–5; 5:14),[2] and

2. While the 1 Timothy 3 passage is directed to elders, we recognize that these spiritual leaders are to set an example for all men. The call to manage one's household well is a qualification for eldership, so it is expected that men in general are to do likewise.

therefore both should be involved in making decisions about the home. The home is something they build together and should reflect both of their personalities, interests, concerns, and aspirations.

Second, there are situations where male headship may help us resolve some tension in decision-making, but such situations should be rare. Couples will have disagreements, but generally they should be able to discuss those disagreements, problem-solve together, and come to some sort of solution or compromise. If you are facing lots of unresolvable conflict, then it may indicate that you and your spouse need to work on your shared family vision.[3] You should rarely have to invoke headship to resolve a disagreement.

Lastly, whenever a husband uses headship to help settle a dispute, he is borrowing on the trust his wife has in him. To exercise headship in decision-making is to ask your wife to trust you. In such moments, husbands are making a withdrawal from their wives' relational account. This can be appropriate when the decision is a weighty one and isn't simply about your preferences. The rarer these types of situations are, the easier it is for a wife to trust a headship decision. If, however, headship decisions are used for every manner of disagreement, then trust will quickly be depleted. In this case, your wife will feel as though you are using headship not for her good but for selfish gain.[4] For example, if a couple cannot decide where to go on vacation, how to spend their tax refund, or where to eat out for dinner, and the husband consistently makes the final decision because "I am the man," then this will quickly destroy his wife's trust in him. These are not the

3. See chapter 3 of this book: "A Shared Family Vision."

4. For more on this, we recommend Brad Hambrick, *Decision-Making: Listening Guide*, Creating a Gospel-Centered Marriage IV (The Summit Church, 2013), 45. Available online at https://bradhambrick.com/wp-content/uploads/2015/05/GCM_Decision-Making_Listening-Guide_2.0.pdf.

kinds of decisions for which headship needs to be exercised, and they tend to result in a husband simply justifying his preferences.

THE PROVERBS 31 HUSBAND

The Bible presents us with a compelling example of a husband who models power under instead of power over. Proverbs 31 portrays a godly woman and describes her various attributes, attitudes, and accomplishments. It is exceedingly popular in Christian circles today to encourage women to be a "Proverbs 31 wife." But the text also lends us a few insights about her empowering husband.

Proverbs 31:10–31 can be described as an epilogue to the entire book, one concerned with the "wife of noble character." The text describes this woman from a number of vantage points: her productivity, her sense of responsibility, her care for her family, her business savvy, her generosity to the poor, her preparedness, her wisdom, and her fear of the Lord. But let's explore what all these noble characteristics reveal about her husband.

The first phrase we see that gives us insight about the woman's husband is a direct reference to him: "Her husband has full confidence in her" (v. 11, NIV). The ESV states, "The heart of her husband trusts in her." The word *heart* is important here. The Hebrew word that we translate as "heart" can refer to emotions, intellect, or will. It's a robust word that communicates the husband's deep confidence and trust. The verse adds that this man "lacks nothing of value" (NIV), meaning he is not afraid of what will happen in his marriage. He's not worried about what she will do, or where she will go, or what consequences will come to him as a result of her activities. He has full intellectual and emotional confidence in her.

The husband's lack of concern speaks to her "noble character," but it also speaks to his trust in that character. He doesn't micromanage her, monitor her activity, critique her, or evaluate her decisions. He trusts her. He is willing to let her exercise her noble character apart from his involvement. He fully supports her, and she senses that; as a result she lives with freedom.

The Proverbs 31 woman is given the freedom to lead as she thinks best. She is able to use her skills, her wisdom, and her awareness to care for her family. Her husband trusts her to do this and gives her the latitude to make decisions. She gets "wool and flax" (v. 13), she buys a field, she plants a vineyard (see v. 16). There's no hint in the text that she must ask his permission, get his approval, or wait on him to make decisions. She is assertive, intelligent, and capable. A Proverbs 31 husband supports his wife's decision-making abilities and her competence to assess situations. The fact that this woman buys a field and plants a vineyard is no small thing. She demonstrates some real business acumen: She evaluates a field, determines its worth, and buys it. "She perceives that her merchandise is profitable," says verse 18. She is not merely carrying out the duties of a domestic life. She is doing business. She is assessing, buying, and evaluating her profit. Her Proverbs 31 husband doesn't limit her activities to specific domestic tasks; he honors the breadth of her interests, intellect, and skill. Furthermore, he has created such stability in their home that she can freely make these decisions without fear of repercussions.

The woman's husband is again mentioned in verse 23. He is known at the city gates among the elders, we are told. This reflects that he is a man of status and influence. Yet he doesn't throw these things around to manage his wife or overrule her in the family dynamic. He trusts her completely. He is not afraid of being embarrassed. He is not so insecure that he needs to be involved in all of her tasks and choices. He has confidence that she will be able to fulfill her roles and represent their family well in so doing. Her competence is not a threat to his status. Rather, in verses 28–29 he praises her. A Proverbs 31 husband respects, honors, and affirms his wife's value and work. She senses that, despite his status, he is not going to lord it over her and undercut her decisions.

Are you a Proverbs 31 husband? Do you trust your wife with full confidence, both intellectually and emotionally? Do you support her work, affirming and honoring her value? Do you give her latitude to make choices and manage the household well? Do you recognize her worth beyond the domestic duties of a wife and mother?[5] A Proverbs 31 husband does all these things, so take some time to evaluate yourself and see if you fit this mold.

CONCLUSION

A husband's role as spiritual leader involves the key principles of safety, support, and stability. The Proverbs 31 husband gives us a good model of what those principles look like in practice. Power under should empower wives for godliness and life. Husbands do have a leadership role in the family, but that role is most clearly fulfilled by "living with your wife in an understanding way." So, how well do you understand your wife?

QUESTIONS FOR A HUSBAND'S REFLECTION

1. Of the three key principles outlined in this chapter (safety, support, and stability), which do you feel the strongest in? Which do you feel the weakest in?

5. We are not claiming here that all women should be stay-at-home wives, nor are we suggesting that men should not be involved in domestic duties.

2. In what ways do you reflect the Proverbs 31 husband? In what ways do you not reflect the Proverbs 31 husband?
3. Evaluate how well you understand your wife (1= low; 10 = high). Ask your wife to evaluate you using this same scale. If your answers differ, discuss them with each other.
4. Take time to ask your wife this week about her greatest joys, greatest fears, greatest hopes, and most unfulfilled dreams. What can you do to care for and support her in light of her answers to those questions?

5

A WIFE'S USE OF POWER

Emma sat silently at the dinner table, nodding along as her husband made a decision. She felt his choice would hurt their family in the long run, but she wasn't going to say anything. It was not the first time she had remained silent about legitimate concerns, believing that submission meant keeping her thoughts and opinions to herself. Gradually, her voice disappeared from their marriage altogether as she physically and emotionally faded into the background.

Meanwhile, Lisa operated very differently within her marriage. Raised to have strong opinions, she made sure her husband knew all of them. If he hesitated or did not fully agree in any way, she pushed harder, ensuring that her methods and ideas won out. He tended to be quieter and more contemplative. She got frustrated when she had to wait on him to make a decision. In her opinion, their marriage worked better if she just did everything. Though she didn't really ask him, he never complained about it, so she assumed he agreed with her anyway.

Both of these women had failed to understand the proper way to be helpers to their husbands, mainly because the concept of submission was misplaced within their marriages. Because of this, each of them had developed an unhealthy relationship with her husband due to a poor view of her role.

When a wife overemphasizes submission, she can become a doormat, losing her overall influence in her husband's life. Her husband suffers because he is not positively impacted by her distinctive and God-given experiences, talents, character, and voice. But when she neglects to harness or control her influence well, she can steamroll his authority. This may sway his mind in unhelpful ways, ignoring the part that submission plays in her role. One primary way to address this dilemma is to reestablish the central theme of a wife's role by moving away from submission as the comprehensive guiding concept. Doing so can renew the distribution of power within marriage, allowing a wife's influence (and thus a husband's authority) to function as God intended.

A BETTER DESCRIPTION

Helper is the most accurate term to encapsulate a wife's role because it is the word that God initially used to describe Eve, the model for all the wives who would follow. It captures the fullness of her design without distortion. She is neither diminished into insignificance nor inflated into a role of domination; rather, she is one who comes alongside her husband with indispensable strength.

Other terms may highlight parts of her role, but only *helper* holds together all the dimensions of who God made a wife to be. It reflects his intention from creation, it conveys the abundant contributions a wife makes to the marriage, and it corresponds to God's character as our helper who is full of power. To embrace this role is not to settle for less but to embody God's highest and most truthful description of womanhood.

God recognized that man should not be alone and created a helper suited for him (see Gen. 2:18). The woman was designed to help the man accomplish God's purposes for them both. Accordingly, the help that a wife offers is not meant to meet her husband's needs so much as it is meant to reflect the oneness and unity required to complete their shared purpose.

Though God had created many useful creatures before he created Eve, none could fulfill the role of helper for man. So, God created a "suitable helper," not as inferior or secondary but as necessary to complete the tasks he had prepared for husband and wife together. Thus, the term *helper* best captures the wife's God-given role—not as an afterthought or the lesser partner but as an intentional and essential provision of God from the very beginning of creation.

Unlike the heading of *submission*, all of the other biblical commands and instructions a wife is given in Scripture naturally fall under the umbrella of helper. A wife's role encompasses a broad range of responsibilities, so the word used to describe it should convey its extensive nature. Grounding a wife's role in the term *helper* even widens its scope to include the instructions she should already be living out as a member of the body of Christ, as a child in the family of God, and as a part of the human race. After all, marriage doesn't narrow a woman's role; it expands it. She isn't exempt from all the other commands of Scripture so that she can focus on being a wife. Rather, she needs to understand how these general instructions fit within her marital relationship. A well-rounded view of her role should include the whole counsel of God, not just the verses that apply solely to wives. To call her a helper is to recognize the breadth of her role, one that cannot be reduced to a single task or erase the commands she had already been given before marriage.

The term *helper* is not just accurate and necessary; it also reflects the character of God. People are not prone to think of a helper as powerful, especially when it comes to the role of a wife. She can often be reduced to her husband's assistant, to one who follows behind him, taking care of the mundane tasks that would otherwise keep him from doing "the real work." But all throughout Scripture, God is described as a helper to his people—and he is not a mere assistant to them but the ultimate source of their power and flourishing.[1] He is the only way his people can survive. So, if wives are called by God to be a helper to their husbands, they are not to think of their actions as powerless, weak, or secondary. In embracing this calling, a wife is not diminished; rather, she is entrusted with a role that mirrors God's own powerful and life-giving help.

THE POWER OF INFLUENCE

All throughout Scripture, we see that God has supplied women with the unique power of influence—persuasion that can be used for great good or great harm. In the garden, Eve tragically used her influence to draw Adam into sin (see Gen. 3:6). Later, Delilah manipulated Samson through her persistent nagging (see Judg. 16:15–17). Yet Esther used her influence to move the heart of a king, persuading him to act for justice and protect God's people (see Est. 8:3–8). Such examples show us that women in general

1. See, for example, Exodus 18:4; Psalms 10:14; 27:9; 40:7; 46:1; 54:4; 63:7; 94:17; 118:7; Hebrews 13:6.

have a persuasive hold on men, one that can be dangerous when wielded selfishly but life-giving when used wisely and righteously.

Within marriage, this influence is intensified: Because of the deep intimacy and covenantal trust between husband and wife, a wife is uniquely positioned to shape her husband's choices, often in ways he would not arrive at alone. Her influence is not the same as his authority, but neither is it less powerful. While his authority is expressed through loving guidance and sacrificial care, her influence works through the bonds of intimacy, trust, and persuasion. When a wife uses her influence to encourage righteousness, to strengthen what is good, and to redirect what is harmful, she embodies her God-given role as helper—coming alongside her husband as a partner who strengthens him to walk faithfully before the Lord.

THE CORE PRACTICES OF A HELPER

As a helper himself, God shows a wife how she can carry out her role as helper. He is not only a helper as he strengthens and sustains his people, but through the Holy Spirit, he also helps to sharpen their character. And so, to better understand its meaning and application, the role of helper can be divided into three central practices that reflect the character of God. As a helper, a wife is called to strengthen, sustain, and sharpen within her marriage—in this way leading both her and her husband to flourish.

Strengthen

The Hebrew word *ezer*, translated as "helper" in Genesis 2:18, is also used throughout Scripture to describe the great strength with which God empowers people during difficult times. It speaks of his ability to rescue and care for those who could not continue forward, or even survive, without him. He provides lasting strength and support to those who covenant with him.[2] Helping is a reflection of the strength God brings to a dire situation, and it shows his care for those who need him.

When someone feels they can't go on, it is the borrowed strength from another that lifts them up and carries them forward. This is how a wife should use the gift of strength within her marriage. A wife who is a helper brings life to the hopeless, restoring strength and enabling flourishing.

So, what does it look like for a wife to strengthen her husband? It might mean cultivating hope when the weight of discouragement presses in. A wife can use her special gift of influence to persuade her husband to believe truth when he's surrounded by lies. A wife can speak Scripture to him—reminding her husband of the character of God and the promises God has made—because the best help she can offer comes from God's own words. When her husband is burdened by setbacks, criticism, or fear of the future, what he needs is not more panic and pressure but a steady voice of influential truth.

This doesn't mean that you can't share your own frustrations and disappointments as a wife, but by continually reminding your husband of God's past faithfulness and the sure hope we have in Christ, you can give him the courage to keep going. In moments when his strength runs dry (after losing his job, when he is facing a long-term illness, when the consequences of a bad decision are weighing on him, and so on), your calm reassurance becomes the strength he can borrow—helping him to endure, and even flourish, when he might otherwise have given up.

2. In fact, in the Bible, *ezer* is used to describe God more often than it's used to describe people.

Another dimension of a wife's role as helper is the call to courage in moments of crisis. Scripture never confines strength and protection exclusively to husbands; rather, Scripture presents courage as a virtue rooted in one's trust in God, and so it is available to all his people. While a husband might bring courage through his leadership, a wife might do the same through her power of influence. Esther exemplifies such encouraging influence when she risks her life to preserve God's covenant community (see Est. 4:16).

In this light, a wife who steadies herself in faith during seasons of fear participates in God's design for mutual strength within marriage. Her courage is not a negation of her husband's leadership but a complementary reflection of the Helper-God himself, who strengthens his people in their weakness (see Ps. 46:1). By living with such Spirit-empowered courage, a wife provides tangible strength to her husband, anchoring him in God's sovereign care and demonstrating that true security comes not from man-made roles but from God's steadfast presence.

A wife can also show strength by admitting her human frailty and inviting her husband to share her responsibilities in times of trial. After all, God intended that marriage partners provide *mutual* help, and if the wife thinks she is only to give and never to receive help, she will become isolated, overwhelmed, and exhausted. Rather than spiraling in ways that disrupt the unity of the marriage, she should remember that true strength is found not in proving herself and carrying every burden alone but in humbly using her voice to express her limits and seek support. In doing so, she reminds her husband that "[God's] power is perfected in weakness" (see 2 Cor. 12:9–10) and that her strength and power are produced not by her own resolution but by God's mighty hand. And as she draws her husband into her areas of need, they learn to walk the way of humility and mutual sacrifice together. A wife who shares her needs displays strength because she points to the power of God and encourages unity in her marriage.

Finally, a wife can strengthen her husband by honing and applying the skill of discernment. If a wife is to influence the decisions and direction of her husband and family, she must be careful what information she relies on for guidance. She can protect her family from situations that may harm their faith, incite social conflict, or deplete emotional stamina—but only if she exercises great spiritual and practical discernment.

A woman's intuition is very real, a unique part of her biological makeup. Research shows that women, on average, score higher than men when tested on emotional intelligence and nonverbal sensitivity;[3] according to scans of their brains, certain parts respond differently to these types of stimuli.[4] It seems that they were made to provide this type of strength. Just as Abigail recognized a threat and was able to undo tensions to protect her family (see 1 Sam. 25), a wife can use her insight and discernment to create a safe and godly environment. Heeding subtle cues, she can be alert to false teaching, unhealthy relationships, or destructive habits.

A helper does not simply allow her husband to take the spiritual reins; rather, she studies and applies the Word in a way that supports and builds on what he knows and, when necessary, corrects and challenges him when she believes he is wrong. She shares

3. Agneta H. Fischer, Mariska E. Kret, and Joost Broekens, "Gender Differences in Emotion Perception and Self-Reported Emotional Intelligence: A Test of the Emotion Sensitivity Hypothesis," *PLOS ONE* 13, no. 1 (2018), doi: 10.1371/journal.pone.0190712.

4. Jennifer S. Stevens and Stephan Hamann, "Sex Differences in Brain Activation to Emotional Stimuli: A Meta-Analysis of Neuroimaging Studies," *Neuropsychologia* 50, no. 7 (2012): 1578–93, doi: 10.1016/j.neuropsychologia.2012.03.011.

her hunches and observations because they could be the very means God uses to protect her husband from a harmful decision or to redirect him toward wisdom. When offered with humility and love, her discernment improves on and strengthens her husband's perspective rather than competing with it, allowing them to walk forward together in greater unity. In this way, a wife's intuition and spiritual attentiveness become not a challenge to her husband's authority but a vital expression of her calling as a helper—guarding her home and strengthening their shared pursuit of Christ.

Sustain

Strength takes the spotlight in moments of crisis, but sustaining acts, though tedious and often unseen, give life its lasting shape. To sustain is to create rhythms of love, patience, and daily care—to quietly uphold one's responsibilities with faithfulness and grace. Such work, like the power of influence in general, rarely draws applause. Yet it is the very soil in which all endeavors take root. Even the boldest plans will wither if they are not supported by steady endurance.

Scripture gives us a glimpse of this endurance in the form of the woman of Proverbs 31. Her diligence day by day allows her household to flourish. In this steadfast service, a wife reflects the sustaining grace of God himself—the grace by which all creation continues and holds together.

One way a wife can sustain her husband is by celebrating his growth and his victories. In this way she influences what he believes about himself, God, others, and the world around him. It is difficult for anyone to persevere in daily work or ministry when no one acknowledges their accomplishments. Whether a husband's vocation is in the public eye, quietly hidden in an office, or devoted to the home, his work is sustained when his wife notices and affirms his effort. Even if he doesn't always express appreciation for it, something deep within a husband's heart is strengthened when his wife cheers him on.

Although a wife is not called to be her husband's forever cheerleader, praising his actions no matter what they may be, she is called to have a posture that encourages him and builds him up (see 1 Thess. 5:11). Noticing her husband's spiritual progress not only helps him recognize the Spirit's work in his life but also gives him courage for the next step of sanctification. When a wife celebrates her husband's victories, both great and small, she sustains him with the kind of encouragement that steadies his soul and propels him toward God's calling for both of them.

In addition to celebrating her husband, a wife can create an environment of intimacy and joy by cultivating family rhythms. That doesn't necessarily require that she is physically present for every moment of every activity, but by intentionally influencing the patterns and priorities that shape her family, she can foster an atmosphere of consistency, not control. Even if she works outside the home, she can help establish daily and weekly anchors that give her marriage and family a sense of stability.

This might be as simple as setting times for shared meals, praying as a family in the morning or evening, planning a Sabbath rest, or building small rituals of connection into your days, such as naming one thing you are grateful for each day, walking after dinner, or playing video games together. When our kids were younger, we had a ritual that we simply called "Family Night." Every Monday evening, we took turns deciding what we would do as a family. But even if children aren't in the picture, it is important for a wife to encourage basic rhythms and rituals with her husband that help sustain their intimacy and keep their marriage fun.

Proverbs 31 presents a woman who both excels in business and cares for her household. Her strength lies not in doing everything herself but in stewarding her resources, ordering her life with wisdom, and ensuring that her family flourishes under her care. A wife can do the same by setting rhythms that align with her family's values and that point them back to the Lord. She doesn't need to carry the burden alone—mutuality in marriage means her husband should help create and sustain these rhythms as well. In the end, what shapes the home is not necessarily the number of hours spent there but the intentionality invested in them. By weaving practices of worship, connection, and rest into her family's schedule, a wife fosters an atmosphere that sustains her household, even if her other responsibilities take her beyond its walls.

Lastly, a wife can use her power to sustain her marriage by providing a space for open communication and reciprocal burden-bearing. She can create a culture of vulnerability not by having all the right answers but by admitting faults and offering forgiveness, making it safe for her husband to open up to her. She can influence the atmosphere in her marriage through example. Paul urges believers to "bear one another's burdens, and so fulfill the law of Christ" (Gal. 6:2 ESV). That begins at home. When a wife listens without rushing in to fix the problem, criticizes less and encourages more, and resists the urge to weaponize her husband's struggles, she is building a refuge where he can let down his guard. Vulnerability thrives where respect and grace are consistently displayed.

Practically speaking, this might mean that a couple set aside regular times to check in with each other emotionally, asking open-ended questions like "How are you dealing with stress this week?" or "What has been weighing most heavily on you these days?" You can make it a ritual to share the worst and best part of each day, being sensitive to which time is best for sharing deeply and honestly without feeling rushed. During these times, husband and wife can practice responding with empathy rather than judgment, saying,

"I can see that's been really hard for you—how can I walk through that with you?" instead of offering quick solutions.

Creating such a space does not mean a wife never shares her own hurts or concerns. In fact, her sincerity and honesty model the very kind of vulnerability she hopes to see in her husband. By taking the risk to reveal her own burdens, she invites him into the shared experience of mutual care. In this way, communication becomes less about fixing problems and more about walking side by side, lifting together what neither could carry alone.

Sharpen

Finally, a wife can fulfill her role as helper not only by standing beside her husband in the practical rhythms of life but also by entering into the deeper work of nurturing his heart and faith. Just as iron sharpens iron (see Prov. 27:17), a wife shapes and refines her husband by sharing her wisdom, perspective, and insights. Even the wisest man is blind to his own weaknesses; each of our hearts is "more deceitful than anything else, and incurable" (Jer. 17:9).

On top of that, pride, discouragement, and weariness can dull our discernment. A wife sees from a different vantage point than her husband and thus should speak truth in love when temptation leads him to drift and call him back to faithfulness when his steps falter. Far from undermining his leadership, her acts of sharpening positively influence his ability to lead. A leader who is teachable, prayerfully supported, and lovingly challenged will serve his family more faithfully.

Ultimately, a husband needs sharpening because marriage itself is designed to be sanctifying. God uses husband and wife together to chisel away selfishness and to stir each other toward Christlikeness. A wife who embraces this calling helps her husband become more of the man God intends him to be—not for her sake alone but for the flourishing of the whole family and the glory of God.

In order to sharpen her husband, a wife must seek to offer wise counsel. Her voice is vital to him because she brings insight and perspective into conversations and decision-making. Just as Abigail's wise intervention saved her household (see 1 Sam. 25:18–35), a wife's input can make the difference between joyful flourishing and disastrous chaos within her family. Her words, offered in wisdom and love, can be the edge that keeps her husband from growing dull, guiding him to the path of eternal life. But in order for her counsel to be right and true, her thoughts must be shaped by God's Word. Reading, meditating, and memorizing Scripture will allow her to be reliable and trustworthy, which will in turn encourage her husband to seek her guidance.

One of the most powerful ways a wife can sharpen her husband is by praying for him and with him. This kind of prayer is not merely a private act of devotion but a form of partnership, one in which she seeks God's wisdom, protection, and blessing on his life. In prayer, a wife's knowledge of Scripture guides her requests, helping shape both her own heart and his toward God's truth. When she lifts her husband before the Lord, she offers encouragement that words alone cannot provide—reminding him that he isn't carrying life's burdens on his own. When she joins him in prayer, she strengthens their unity, creating a space where both are humbled together before God's authority.

Consider setting aside a few minutes before bed to pray together about the stresses of the day or texting your husband a short passage of Scripture and a prayer during his workday. These simple habits remind him that his life and leadership are upheld by God's strength, not his own, and they invite him to join you in depending on the Lord.

A wife also sharpens her husband by remaining faithful in her own walk with Christ. Her steady devotion—seen in her commitment to Scripture, her perseverance in prayer, and her obedience in everyday life—becomes a living testimony that quietly influences and challenges her husband. Just as Paul urged Timothy to "set an example for the believers in speech, in conduct, in love, in faith, and in purity" (1 Tim. 4:12), so a wife's faithfulness points her husband toward greater devotion. Her integrity under pressure, her trust in God amid difficult circumstances, and her willingness to keep serving even when unnoticed all model what it means to follow Christ.

By watching his wife's faith at work, a husband is sharpened—reminded of the hope they share and inspired to walk more faithfully himself. He can be won without a word by the faithful, respectful, and pure conduct of his wife (see 1 Peter 3:1–2). Even small acts, like faithfully attending church week after week or selflessly caring for their children, remind him by example that faith is not about fleeting feelings but about steady trust in God. In these ways, her lived faithfulness sharpens his own.

Finally, a wife can be a faithful helper to her husband by speaking the truth in love. This means gently confronting him when he veers into sin and calling him back to the wisdom of God. Nathan's confrontation of David (see 2 Sam. 12) gives us a powerful picture of how God uses truth spoken in love to restore.

In marriage, this might look like a wife noticing her husband's growing bitterness toward a coworker and saying, "I can see how much this situation is weighing on you, but I also see the anger building in your heart. How can I pray for you as you work through this?" Such words are meant not to tear down but to build up, helping him remember God's call to holiness and grace. As Paul instructs, we are to "encourage one another and build each other up" (1 Thess. 5:11), reflecting the God who comforts the downcast even when their own sin has brought them low (see 2 Cor. 7:6).

A WORD ABOUT SUBMISSION

We have not said much about submission up to this point, but we must. A wife is indeed called to submit to her husband, but this is only one aspect of a much larger calling. When submission is pulled out of its proper context and made the centerpiece of marriage, the balance of power is distorted, and God's design is misrepresented.

Scripture presents submission not as blind obedience or as the defining feature of a wife's role but as one expression within a relationship of mutual love, respect, and service. Sadly, when people exaggerate its importance or misunderstand its meaning, wives and marriages can suffer harm. To focus on submission without foregrounding the broader call to companionship, mutual encouragement, and a shared pursuit of Christ is to miss the beauty of what God intended marriage to be. True submission can be understood rightly only when it is seen as part of a larger picture, one in which both husband and wife seek to help each other flourish in the Lord.

Yet God has placed men in a position of leadership within the home, and Scripture expressly and repeatedly commands women to submit to their husbands (see Eph. 5:22–24;[5] Col. 3:18; Titus 2:5; 1 Peter 3:1, 5). Though husbands are called to die to themselves for the sake of their wives, and though both men and women are called to submit to one another (implying that husbands also

5. Although the word *submit* is not found in verse 22, it is implied by the structure of the grammar. The verb of the sentence is implied from the verb in the preceding verse.

submit), God's Word does say there is something unique about the submission of a wife to her own husband. There is a way in which this submission honors the leadership structure that God has established. In this sense, then, a wife submits ultimately to God's authority, not to her husband's. But, because so much confusion and potential danger surrounds this idea, we should strive to understand what submission is and what it isn't.

There is an important difference between the posture and practice of submission. Scripture describes submission as a heart posture that reflects a wife's attitude toward her husband's God-given role in the home (see Eph. 5:22–24). It is first and foremost an *orientation of the heart*, marked by respect, trust, and a willingness to support her husband's leadership. This posture does not mean a wife is constantly deferring her will or setting aside her power in every situation. Rather, it means she approaches the marriage relationship with a readiness to work in harmony with her husband's leadership, not in opposition to it. Therefore, submission is an orientation of a wife's heart that is expressed through the purposeful yielding of her power in specific situations in which her husband asks for her trust. Let's break down our definition piece by piece.

First, submission is a purposeful yielding of a wife's power. Wives are not powerless; God has given them real power and responsibility, just as he has husbands. They are called to use that power for their husbands' good and for the flourishing of their homes. At times, a wife may choose to *yield*—that is, to defer the exercise of her power to her husband's leadership in a specific matter. This yielding is not a forfeiting of power but a voluntary act of trust and partnership. It is a deliberate and discerning choice made from strength, not weakness.

To submit, in other words, is not the same as to be dominated. Domination takes power away; true submission offers it willingly.

A wife who is being oppressed is not freely yielding her power—it is being taken from her. True submission arises from a willing heart and cannot be forced.

Second, submission is expressed by a purposeful act in a particular situation. The practical expression of this posture takes shape in specific, limited moments—when differing perspectives arise, when decisions must be made, and when her husband must take responsibility before God for the direction of their home. In such instances, she may *yield* the exercise of her power, not because she lacks it, but because she willingly chooses to trust and support her husband's leadership in that particular moment. Her submission is demonstrated therefore not as a continual silencing of her voice or autonomy; it is a discerning, voluntary alignment of her heart and actions in particular contexts.

If a wife is regularly "overruled" by her husband, constantly submitting to decisions with which she disagrees, then it likely means that there is not a shared vision for life and that there is a misunderstanding about gender roles in marriage. When a husband and wife have spent time understanding each other, building a unified life together, and casting a vision for their shared life, these moments of practiced submission will be rare. True submission, then, is not about erasing a wife's voice. Rather, it is about showing trust in moments of tension, so that the unity of the marriage is preserved and the purposes of God are advanced.

Third, submission is a yielding of a wife's power in response to her husband's request for trust. That's ultimately what a headship decision is: a request for trust. It is a husband borrowing on his relational capital with his wife and asking her to yield to him in a specific situation, to trust his judgment over her preferences. This means submission is not about blind obedience or unquestioning compliance; it is about relational trust built over time through love, care, and consistency. A call to submit, then, should cause a wife to ask herself, "Can I trust my husband in this moment? Has he shown himself to be a man who seeks the Lord, who listens to my voice, and who desires our unity more than his own way?" If so, submission becomes an act of love that strengthens the marriage bond rather than diminishing it.

But if a husband is not trustworthy—if he has established a pattern of disregarding his wife's voice, acting selfishly, and regularly misusing his authority—his wife has reason to seek outside help for the health of the marriage. Scripture never endorses submission to sin, abuse, or coercion. Submission is a call to trust, but when that trust has been violated, abused, or misused, a wife ought to seek wise counsel and protection for herself, as well as accountability for her husband. True biblical submission rests on the foundation of mutual love and trust; without that foundation, the call itself becomes distorted and dangerous. To refrain from submitting in those circumstances and seek help may be most faithful to God and to the marriage covenant.

When submission is misunderstood, often the practical outworking is a wife's reluctance to question her husband's authority or confront his sin in order to protect his reputation. But speaking up about one's preferences, contributing one's ideas, and correcting one's spouse should never be considered a negative part of marriage or interpreted as a "lack of submission." Addressing sin and mistakes is not an act of resistance but an expression of genuine support.

If you avoid hard conversations out of fear that your words will undermine your husband's authority, you are actually calling into question the strength of that authority. If his authority is not strong enough to withstand some critique, it is not very strong. This type of weakness can lead to a relationship built on apprehension rather than mutual growth. True confidence in your husband's leadership is demonstrated when you can lovingly and respectfully call him to repentance and grace, trusting that a strong and godly leader welcomes truth and accountability.

In a sense, submission could fit under any of the three categories listed above. Submission lends *strength* to the system of marital power that God has designed. Both husband and wife are strengthened by the way submission brings order to their power. Submission also helps a wife *sustain* her husband. When she trusts in his ability to make difficult choices in which there is no clear and unanimous decision, she can help his leadership be sustained more effectively over time. And submission can allow a wife to *sharpen* her husband by stressing his need to steward her trust. Submission challenges a husband to use his power to hold her up. It calls him to provide support, safety, and stability as he leads. It calls him to make choices that honor her and promote her well-being.

Ultimately, submission is just one part of a wife's role, and it is not even the most important. Scripture does teach wives to submit to their husbands in a unique way, but we should not overemphasize submission in marriage. A robust view of the wife's power helps us see that she has so much more to offer and so much more to do in marriage.

QUESTIONS FOR A WIFE'S REFLECTION

1. Of the three characteristics of a wife's use of power (strengthen, sustain, and sharpen), which do you feel strongest in? Why? Which do you feel weakest in? Why?
2. How did this chapter perhaps alter your understanding of the concept of "submission"? How might drawing a

distinction between the posture and the practice of submission be important?

3. How can you practically use your power this week to be a helper to your husband?
4. How can viewing your role as "helper" instead of "submitter" be healthier for your marriage and more honoring to the Lord?

6

THE MUTUAL APPLICATION OF POWER IN MARRIAGE

Husbands and wives both have power. Both are called by God to serve each other with that power in such a way that it enables their mutual flourishing. We come, then, to one final set of practices that can help husbands and wives use their power to bless each other: collaboration, companionship, and consideration. These three practices are not commonly discussed in marriage literature, but they truly are essential to properly stewarding power in marriage.

COLLABORATION

First, let's consider the concept of collaboration. Collaboration describes the way a husband and wife should work together to make plans for their lives as they complete everyday tasks and set long-term goals. Each spouse uses their own gifts, abilities, upbringing, and experiences to create a new family that honors God to the best of their ability. Collaboration brings unity, it builds up husband and wife in love and good works, and it reflects the reality of two becoming one flesh. To help us better understand what marital collaboration is, we can start by explaining what it is not.

What Collaboration Is Not: Cooperation

We often use the words *cooperation* and *collaboration* interchangeably. But we can see a subtle difference between them—especially when describing how marital roles are carried out. While both words describe ways of working together to achieve a shared goal, *cooperation* connotes a rigid distribution of tasks according to predetermined and fixed criteria. When two people cooperate, they handle separate aspects of a project, then bring them together for a common purpose.

An example of cooperation in a marriage relationship is the strict division of chores solely according to gender and related stereotypical roles. Within this system, a wife assumes all the responsibility for cooking, cleaning, and doing laundry, based on the assumption that domestic chores should be reserved for women. Since the whole family eats, makes messes, and requires clean clothes each day, the wife can feel consistently overworked and tied down to the home.

When such a wife is in an exceptionally trying season of life and her chores pile up, she may think that her choice is either to press on to exhaustion or to watch her house be consumed by disarray. If her husband has less work during a given season, he will not necessarily pick up any extra chores if he doesn't consider them to be within his designated category. In fact, it is common for husbands in homes like this not to know how to cook, clean, or do laundry, and so the whole system begins to break down if the wife gets sick or becomes incapacitated in some way.

This type of cooperation fails to consider the ways in which life and people change. Forcing broad categories of responsibilities upon someone because of their gender doesn't recognize their personal limitations, interests, or abilities. Nor does it consider seasons of life in which adjustments might need to be made.

When cooperation is rigid, predetermined, and fixed, both husband and wife have less flexibility. Although they share a goal, they perform their individual tasks more or less independently of each other. As a marital mindset, cooperation does not establish the best framework for cultivating unity and mutuality. It doesn't afford as much room for each spouse to use their individual power to pursue reciprocal flourishing.

The Advantages of Collaboration

Collaboration is a much more valuable mindset because it requires the give-and-take of mutuality. It doesn't rely on a cookie-cutter method for determining who performs what tasks. Collaborators can accomplish their shared goal in a way that reflects their unique gifts, talents, and abilities. Further, collaboration allows for each person's individuality to determine how they contribute to the overall goal. It encourages organic adjustments so that no one is left with drastically more work than another and so that there aren't as many breaks in the system when something changes. The fluid nature of collaboration makes it possible to accomplish the original goal even when things don't go as planned.

As a marital framework, collaboration acknowledges that gifts and abilities may or may not align with gender norms, so husbands and wives can be flexible when they consider how to divide tasks between them. Each spouse has a unique combination of interests, skills, abilities, experiences, and ideas that God has sovereignly given them over the course of their life before marriage. Ideally, they will find a way to incorporate these things into their shared life as they seek to achieve the common goals that are established by Scripture (namely, to glorify God and reflect his image, to be fruitful and multiply, to subdue the earth, to love God and love others, to share the gospel, and so on). A collaborative approach recognizes not only that each individual has their own unique contribution to offer but also that every couple has been given diverse resources to accomplish these goals.

Unlike rigid cooperation, collaboration enhances other areas of marital health. Collaboration requires unity—spouses keep peace and reject strife, all while recognizing the other's power and using their own power to help their spouse succeed. Collaboration involves encouragement—spouses lift each other up, understand each other, and don't envy each other. And collaboration entails instruction—spouses teach each other, speak truth to each other, and admonish each other in a spirit of humility. Together these key elements (unity, encouragement, and instruction) can help us better capture the distinct qualities of collaboration.

Collaboration demonstrates unity. Collaboration presents a picture of the unity that husbands and wives are already given in Christ and through which they are called to grow as they increase in holiness over the course of their lives. As members of the body of Christ, we are to be "in full accord and of one mind" (Phil. 2:2 ESV) as we are one in him (see Gal. 3:28). This does not mean that husband and wife have to fully agree with each other on everything. Rather, it means that each spouse should move toward the other, seeking meaningful compromise for the sake of the family.

Moreover, using our talents, abilities, and callings should not only serve one another but also draw us closer together. Just as God gave gifts within the church to build up the body and promote unity in faith (see Eph. 4:12–13), the gifts he has given within marriage are meant to strengthen the couple's shared life. This means our first concern when using our gifts should be how they advance our common goals, not how they fulfill our personal ambitions.

Collaboration may also mean resisting rigid categories of "who does what" at home, so that spouses' strengths are applied to the areas where they serve the family most effectively. For example, if a wife excels in finances and her husband has a talent for repairs, their gifts might play out in different but equally God-honoring ways: She could use her skills in a career while he cares for the home, or she could manage the household budget while he works as a contractor. Neither path is inherently sinful when pursued with a heart to honor God and love others. Marital unity deepens when couples view their strengths not as tools for self-advancement but as means to serve their shared calling in Christ.

Our first major experience with this came when I (Krista) considered going back to school. After our first book, *Table for Two*, gained some attention, I realized I lacked the training to steward new opportunities well. I went to seminary, and David took on more responsibilities at home—cooking, cleaning, and even bringing our toddler to the office on slower days. We enrolled her in preschool the following year, which was helpful for me and enriching for her. Along the way, David discovered that he actually liked to cook and that doing laundry gave him space to clear his head.

After I completed my master's degree, I was able to launch my own biblical counseling business, which has blessed our family in many ways. Although success alone does not prove that something has been done right, this season taught us that living according to rigid, man-made rules can keep us chained to burdens that God never meant for us. When we look up from those chains and ask how our gifts can best serve our spouses and our shared calling, we find greater unity and flourishing.

Collaboration involves encouragement. The unity between a husband and wife means that the outcomes of their shared plans belong to both of them. When the husband succeeds, they both succeed. When the wife flourishes, they both flourish. As they work together toward a shared goal, they can rejoice as they get closer to achieving it together.

After Rex and Simone graduated from college, they got married and moved to Kentucky to live near his family. Rex got a job at the elementary school he had attended as a kid. He slowly moved up the ranks, gathering achievements, accolades, and credentials until he became the principal. In the meantime, Simone stayed at home with their three kids, going to the park and planning art projects for them. They both loved what they were doing.

But something started to change. At first Simone thought it was fun when Rex wanted to appear at every school event, but eventually she started to feel like a background character. He had grown up in the area, so many people already knew him. And because the students loved him so much, he was like a celebrity. Simone didn't necessarily feel jealous. She just felt forgotten, unseen, unimportant, and unsupported. She felt lonely.

Eventually, Simone told Rex that she hated feeling so disconnected from what he was doing. His achievements seemed to belong to him and him alone.

Rex's reply shifted her perspective: "I've actually been thinking about this a lot lately. I'm thriving at work because of your encouragement and guidance. The way you care for our home, the way you listen when I'm stressed, the wisdom you bring when I have a hard decision to make—all of it helps me do what I do."

"That's sweet of you to say," she replied sincerely. "I hadn't really considered that. But I think it might have helped if you'd said some of those things sooner. In the future, would you mind letting me in on those thoughts? I guess I just needed to know that my work mattered to you."

"I'm sorry," Rex said. "From now on, I'll try to think about my work and your work as one thing. Maybe we should sit down and really talk through how we can work together toward a shared purpose. I just know that without you all this would completely fall apart. I want to be better at letting other people know how thankful I am for what you do. And perhaps we can talk about something that you might want to work toward. Our life shouldn't be all about me. I am totally willing to give up some things so that you can have something for yourself as well. I just didn't know you felt that way."

Rex and Simone were able to resolve a potential conflict by focusing on encouragement and unity rather than defending their own individual interests. They sought to understand each other, made sure they were both using their unique gifts to serve and strengthen each other, and viewed their work as one. In this way, they ensured they were collaborating instead of cooperating.

Collaboration requires instruction. Collaboration in marriage does not involve one spouse continually dominating the other to bolster their ego. Both spouses should freely offer their insights, in love and humility reminding each other of biblical truths. The genuine, humble desire of each spouse ought to be that the other learn and grow for their benefit and the benefit of the marriage.

Proverbs 31:26 paints the picture of a woman who "opens her mouth with wisdom, and the teaching of kindness is on her tongue." A Christian wife practices instructive collaboration by being strong and assertive when needed, yet always approaching her husband with humility, gentleness, and respect (see 1 Peter 3:15). Through thoughtful questions and wise counsel, she helps him reflect, make better decisions, and grow in maturity—strengthening their shared walk with Christ.

In the same way, a Christian husband treats his wife with humility, gentleness, and respect, taking the initiative to instruct his family in godliness—not by dominating them but by listening to them, encouraging them, and pointing them to Christ.

When both husband and wife speak into each other's lives with this spirit of mutual care, their partnership reflects the beauty of spiritual maturity and the unity of God's design.

Clara and Dale, a couple in their fifties, sought counseling because of a persistent issue in their marriage. Clara was a tenderhearted, soft-spoken, godly woman. She never put herself down, but she didn't think she had much to offer in her marriage beyond quietly cooking, cleaning, and caring for her husband and extended family. Dale, a successful business owner, had a well-known habit of prayer that was a gift to their family, church, and marriage. He was driven, intelligent, outgoing, and dynamic. His personality and intelligence had always made many things effortless for him.

Now Dale was under an immense amount of stress at work, and Clara didn't know how to help him. His business had suffered throughout the recession, but the changes he needed to make were beyond his ability. His instinct was to work harder, read more, and talk to other business owners, but everything he did seemed to be making it worse. Clara and Dale prayed often about the matter, and nothing really seemed amiss between them—that is, until their counselor turned to Dale and asked, "Have you thought about asking your wife?"

The room was silent for a few seconds while Dale looked at the counselor in bewilderment. He finally replied, "Well, no, but what I do just really isn't her thing. She has plenty of activities that keep her busy. I try not to bore her with my work stuff. We have other things we like to talk about together."

"I just feel like you never want me to be involved," Clara began. "I feel like it's your thing and like you don't want me to mess with it. Besides," she turned to the counselor, "he's a natural at all that business stuff. I wouldn't be any help."

Their counselor looked at Dale. "Why don't you give it a try?" she asked. "Turn to Clara and ask her if she knows what might help your business." Dale thought it was a silly exercise. He felt awkward, and he didn't believe it would amount to anything anyway. But he gave it a shot.

"I wanted to help you so badly," Clara said. "I don't like seeing you suffer this way. But I felt silly for thinking that I might be able to consider something that you didn't already know. I've actually been thinking about this for a while. If I were you, I might focus more on building smaller teams, offering leadership opportunities to people who are not as outspoken in the larger group. Your manager, Rick, can be loud and intimidating to those who are naturally quiet. He quickly offers his opinion and doesn't really wait for other suggestions. If you spread that responsibility out to more people, you can lighten the load that is overwhelming you and create more opportunities for collaboration. You have a really good team. They just don't operate like you do. They need a different space where they can safely speak up. They have good ideas, but they feel hesitant to share them . . . at least that's the sense I've gotten from them at staff parties."

Dale was speechless. He hadn't even known that Clara talked at those parties, because she didn't talk like he did. He talked and laughed in large groups while she quietly mingled. "I had honestly been judging you in my heart because of how you talk to people, and I didn't consider that you might see and know different things given your unique vantage point. I will definitely be asking you for more input in the future. That sounds like an excellent idea . . . and not one that even the experts had considered. I even hired a consultant to figure this thing out! Asking you could have saved me so much money!" Dale laughed, and Clara smiled sheepishly.

By offering instruction with clarity and humility, Clara helped Dale not only sharpen his leadership skills but also deepen his understanding of how collaboration could enhance his work and their marriage. What she thought were weaknesses in herself were actually opportunities to offer a different perspective. Dale realized that the challenges weren't his alone to solve and that Clara's voice was a necessary and valuable part of their shared journey.

COMPANIONSHIP

Next, let's consider companionship. We are called to a standard of love and care in all our Christian relationships; we can think of it simply as friendship. Christians look out for one another, we hold one another accountable, we forgive one another, and we influence one another's beliefs and actions. This standard is elevated within marriage.

When you consider all the instructions given specifically to husbands and wives, you begin to see that this particular friendship requires more, not less, of you. As a fellow believer, you should care for your spouse as a friend, but because they are to receive your first and best efforts, your relationship with them should be more closely examined.

The marriage relationship should be held to much higher standards because it involves a much stronger bond and commitment. Marriage is the only friendship to which you are bound for life. It is the only friendship that requires a covenant, and it's the only one of which Scripture says, "What God has joined together, let no one separate" (Mark 10:9). Further, the companionship between a husband and wife is unique because it is the only relationship in which two friends become one flesh. Their bond with each other is the only one that is sealed and consummated with sexual intimacy. Husbands and wives are meant to have a unique and strong companionship that exceeds all their other relationships in order to provide each other with accountability, influence, and commitment. This companionship is held together by love.

Now, at first glance, love and companionship may not seem to fit into a discussion of power dynamics. After all, worldly power has no place for the sacrifice required of true, biblical love and companionship because worldly power is used entirely to promote the self. The power that many of us have most often seen and experienced does not at all match the well-known picture of love painted in 1 Corinthians 13.

But love and companionship have everything to do with power when you consider the person and work of Jesus Christ. He modeled for us an unconditional and impartial love. During his life on earth, he cared for the poor who could give him nothing in return. He prayed for his enemies who wanted him dead. He displayed the ultimate example of love and companionship when he showed that "no one has greater love than this: to lay down his life for his friends" (John 15:13). And yet, when Jesus died for us, we weren't actually his friends; we were his enemies.

Christ's act of love is a profound act of sacrifice, and so it is the most excellent of examples. He accomplished his saving work without giving up a single ounce of his power. He maintained all his power, but he willingly and lovingly restrained it so that we could be called friends of the most high God.

When we live our lives according to Christ's example, our love should extend to everyone, including our spouses. It should not be conditional, limited, or reserved for moments when our spouses are meeting our expectations. Instead, it should be like the love of Christ—extended freely, sacrificially, and consistently. This means that we must offer grace in times of difficulty, disappointment, or conflict. The love of Christ was not based on circumstantial convenience, and it didn't rely on a swell of emotion. Rather, it was firmly grounded in a commitment to selfless care and sacrifice. Our love for our spouses should mirror that kind of love.

One way to do this is by filtering our intentions and actions through the selfless, sacrificial framework of biblical love. We look to 1 Corinthians 13 for clarity: *As I use my power, am I being patient? Am I being kind? Am I doing so out of envy? Am I seeking to boast? Is this displaying arrogance? Am I being rude? Am I strictly seeking my own way, or am I considering the interest of the other person? Am I being irritable or resentful? Am I rejoicing in truth, or am I sinfully calling attention to my spouse's mistakes?* Following our Lord's example, we use our strengths, influence, and resources to nurture, uplift, and serve others, rather than to dominate or control them.

In marriage, this means that whether we are offering instruction, making decisions, or addressing conflict, we do so with the other person's good at heart. It also means that we do not remain passive when love calls us to act. Love-driven power corrects, protects, and leads with wisdom and grace. By sifting power through love, we ensure that it reflects Christ's example, using whatever strength and influence we have not for selfish ambition but to bring life and blessing to our spouse.

The love between spouses reflects the love that is first and foremost a characteristic of God. When he describes himself, he says he is "merciful and gracious, slow to anger, and abounding in steadfast love" (Ex. 34:6 ESV). To demonstrate that we belong to God, our love for each other should reflect his love for us. As 1 John 4:7–8 tells us,

> Let us love one another, because love is from God, and everyone who loves has been born of God and knows God. The one who does not love does not know God, because God is love.

The love of the triune God is our model; therefore, love within our marriages should be sacrificial and unconditional. We should look for ways to love our spouses—especially when our love is not deserved.

The daily love we demonstrate within our marriages should be covenantal in the sense that it is based on a serious and significant commitment. Marriage vows should not be flippantly made or broken (see Matt. 19:6). Accordingly, our daily choices to love should reflect marital love's deep and profound covenantal origin. We should love with the knowledge that God himself has placed a seal on our wedding vows. This does not mean that we should take our vows lightly, expecting that the covenantal bond will hold everything together for us without any effort on our part. But we also cannot live as if giving up is the first option when love becomes difficult. Real and lasting love involves profound investment and sacrifice, so it must be pursued with the utmost seriousness.

A love like this will color how we exercise and use power. When love is a guiding principle for our use of power, we will not think first and foremost about how to get our own way, how to dominate or control. Instead, we will be asking questions like "How can I use my God-given power to help my spouse thrive?"

CONSIDERATION

Finally, let's explore the practice of consideration. Consideration is the intentional demonstration of care, thoughtfulness, and respect toward one's spouse in daily life. It goes beyond mere politeness and becomes a rhythm of marriage in which each partner actively acknowledges the other's needs, preferences, feelings, and well-being. Consideration has several key characteristics that help us flesh out its practical application within marriage.

Deference

First, each spouse can show consideration to the other through deference. This involves thoughtfully yielding our preferences, desires, or power to support and strengthen our spouses in specific circumstances. In this way we allow our actions to be shaped by the wishes, feelings, or preferences of our spouses.

When Jill's husband, Damon, received a job referral and they mutually decided to move across the country, they had to find a new church. Each worked to evaluate the options. After careful research and visits, they found themselves at a stalemate—Jill preferred one church, while Damon preferred another. After discussing the matter, Jill made the intentional choice to defer to her husband's preference—not because she was obligated to but because she trusted his judgment and valued his leadership. She knew he deeply considered her perspective, had sacrificed for her in other areas, and was committed to their family's spiritual well-being. Her deference in this situation was not about giving up her voice but about prioritizing unity over personal preference.

Similarly, Calvin wanted to change jobs. He was miserable at work and dreamed of starting his own business, but Susie had serious health issues that meant they needed good medical coverage. That was something his "miserable" job provided for them. They discussed the alternatives, and though Susie encouraged Calvin that they would figure it out either way, he knew that he needed to put her needs first. So, he stayed at his job. It meant a lot to Susie to feel like her health was a priority over his career satisfaction. He deferred to her needs over his desires.

Although husbands and wives have the freedom to pursue many opportunities, they must consider how their choices affect their shared life. Deference ought to be a mutual practice in marriage. A husband may adjust his career or lifestyle for his wife's well-being, and a wife can demonstrate love by prioritizing their collective flourishing over her individual ambition.

Deference is also displayed in everyday moments—choosing not to belittle decisions, accommodating preferences in nonessential matters, and addressing disagreements privately rather than confronting each other in public. Specifically, if one spouse struggles with certain behaviors, the other spouse may choose to limit their own freedoms so as not to pose a stumbling block—such as abstaining from alcohol if their spouse battles excessive drinking. In God's kingdom, such acts of humility and love are reflections of the deference of Christ for sinners.

Honor

Second, consideration often entails honor. The apostle Paul encourages believers not merely to honor one another but to actually "outdo one another in showing honor" (Rom. 12:10 ESV). Paul paints a picture of believers almost competing with each other—not for recognition but to outdo each other in showing honor. There is a genuine interest and attentiveness to one another that drives how we relate, connect, and ultimately exercise our power.

Honoring your spouse means seeking to truly understand them—recognizing how God has made them, attending to their emotions, and choosing to act in ways that show genuine care. A husband who honors his wife might decline to participate in a large gathering because he knows she feels overwhelmed in those settings and flourishes more in intimate conversations with a couple of close friends. In the same way, a wife who honors her husband may hold off on resolving an issue right away, recognizing that he needs time to process before he is ready to talk. Both are small but significant ways of saying, "I see you. I value you, and I want to love you as God has made you."

Honor comes in many different forms. It means being attentive to your spouse's feelings—noticing when they are stressed, sad, or angry. It means learning to appreciate and affirm personality differences and personal preferences. It means being thoughtful toward each other, offering kind gestures to demonstrate that you care. It means sacrificing for your spouse, laying aside your interests for the sake of theirs. It means giving each other space to experience emotions differently. Honor means all these things and more. To honor your spouse is to regard them as more important than yourself and to consider their interests along with your own (see Phil. 2:1–4).

When we are committed to honor, it naturally shapes how we use our power in marriage. Honor prompts us to think of the other person first, so that we exercise power not to get our own way but to sacrifice and serve them. In choosing honor, we are denying self and directing our strength toward the good of the one we love. Power in the hands of honor becomes a way to care for others.

Respect

We turn lastly to respect. Too often, respect is spoken of only in relation to husbands and love only in relation to wives. But this is a false dichotomy. Both husbands and wives long to be loved, and both long to be respected. You cannot truly love someone whom you do not also respect. Respect is not a particular need of men; it is the shared longing of every soul created in the image of God.

In marriage, respect takes shape in the way we listen attentively to our spouses and value their insights. It is expressed when we treat each other as image bearers who possess inherent dignity and worth. Respect means recognizing and honoring the individuality of your spouse—the unique ways God has formed and gifted them. It means refusing to belittle them, whether in public or in private, and instead delights in celebrating their character, strengths, and accomplishments.

When respect governs the use of power in marriage, it ensures that every action affirms the equal value of husband and wife. There are no lesser beings within this covenant, no one to dismiss or neglect, no one who stands as secondary. Respect insists that whatever authority or influence we hold, it must be exercised with the unwavering conviction that our spouse is a coheir of grace (see 1 Peter 3:7), an equal partner in calling, and an equivalent contributor in impact. In this way, respect keeps love from becoming sentimental and power from becoming selfish, grounding marriage in the universal dignity God intended from the very beginning.

CONCLUSION

You may have already realized that there are a number of ways in which these particular practices of husbands and wives overlap. We've used different words to describe each practice in order to highlight distinct roles, but in many regards, we are talking about very similar ideas. That's because the basic ways in which we treat other people and live with one another are relevant for all of us. The differences lie more in the manner in which those practices are exercised. Husbands are called to be leaders in the home, and wives are called to be helpers, and that means there are unique ways in which each manifests their role. But there should be plenty of similarity too, because difference in role was never meant to produce division—it was meant to bring unity.

These practices may seem similar because, in one sense, we are all human beings created in the image of the same God, bearing the same dignity, and desiring the same sorts of things from others. We all long for respect, love, support, safety, and companionship. These are not "male needs" or "female needs"; they are human needs.

They may also seem similar because some of these practices are commanded of all Christians. All believers are called to love, to show honor, to protect, and to serve. We are all called to imitate our God, who does these very things with infinite perfection. It should not surprise us, then, to see believing husbands and wives begin to look alike as they both strive to look like Jesus. Their practices overlap because their goal is the same: to reflect him.

And that is the beauty of marriage. Differences in role create unique expressions of leadership and help, but similarities in practice create unity of heart and purpose. Distinction without competition, overlap without confusion—together these allow a marriage to display the fullness of God's design. When both husband and wife commit themselves to Christlike love, they find that their diversity never overshadows their unity.

But neither does their unity overshadow their diversity. The way in which leaders and helpers carry out these practices will necessarily look a bit different, thus the distinct language for each. Yet an overemphasis on differences can lead to a major imbalance in marital power dynamics. A corresponding emphasis on similarity helps us maintain careful boundaries surrounding that imbalance and allows us to pursue oneness and mutuality. Godly power works best in those contexts. After all, power exists to serve others.

It is our differences and our similarities together that allow us to serve each other most fully. That is the model of our Lord and Savior, who, though vastly different from us, "had to be like his brothers and sisters in every way" so that he might meet us in our need and make atonement for our sake (Heb. 2:17). In him we see the truest picture of power—authority laid down in love, strength poured out in service, and honor given to those who least deserved it.

And so, when it comes to power dynamics in marriage, the final word is this: We must look to Jesus, for only when we imitate him will our marriages reflect the beauty of the gospel.

QUESTIONS FOR REFLECTION

1. Of the three mutual applications of power in this chapter (collaboration, companionship, and consideration), which do you feel strongest in? Which do you feel weakest in?
2. What might it look like to pursue collaboration instead of merely cooperation in your marriage? What practical steps can you take to do this?

3. What are some active ways that you can enhance your companionship with your spouse?
4. In what practical ways can you demonstrate deference, respect, and honor to your spouse this week? How can you begin to cultivate this into a habit, not just a once-in-a-while practice?

Appendix A

ADDRESSING MISUSED POWER IN A MARRIAGE

Although we have argued that power is a God-given resource, available to both men and women to be used for the flourishing of all people, power is not distributed equally. God doesn't play by our rules of fairness. What God does do is establish systems that reflect his nature, giving us the opportunity to learn about him and how to be more like him.

And so, in the context of marriage, God has given husbands an innately different kind of power from wives. As the ones with the authority to lead, they have great potential to serve their wives and promote their flourishing, but—ever since sin entered the world—they also have great potential to cause harm through domination. This is why God has also given husbands unique principles and commands to safeguard against abuse.

The misuse of power by a husband has more devastating consequences than when a wife misuses her own power. A wife has the power to influence her husband, and she must guard that. But when a wife uses her influence sinfully, her husband can more easily find a way to escape. He has far more options and resources available to him.[1] When a husband uses his position of authority to sinfully dominate his wife, she has far fewer options. Under the oppression of their husbands' misuse of power, wives often find themselves trapped with no way of escape.

Unfortunately, wives are often taught (directly or indirectly) that they are permitted to challenge their husbands only if a situation has reached "threat level red." Clear barriers must have been plowed over or biblical commands blatantly broken. Over the years, many Christian resources on marriage have implied that a wife may object to her husband's actions only if he is asking her to sin.

The danger in this idea is that if a husband is asking his wife to sin, chances are he has already been sinning for a while before asking his wife to join him. At the least, he has likely made some unwise choices that could have been addressed earlier. Consider a wife who thinks that her husband's choice to invest in a pyramid scheme is unwise but feels unable to say anything about it. She had opportunities to speak up long ago, but a hyperfocus on submission and authority kept her from doing so, and so all their savings are lost.

When a wife keeps silent until sin is committed, innocent people will get hurt. But a wife who learns how to use her power of influence in ways that sharpen her husband and promote mutual flourishing will be more likely to speak up before situations become destructive.

1. Women usually have less access to money than men do. They have fewer opportunities for jobs, especially in positions of influence. And because of their general size and demeanor, they are constantly at a physical and emotional disadvantage. They are on all accounts the "weaker vessel" (see 1 Peter 3:7 ESV).

WHEN YOU NEED TO CONFRONT YOUR HUSBAND

All sin is harmful, but some sins are more harmful than others. Misused power falls on a spectrum. On one end is behavior that approaches misuse (such as dominating the decision-making). On the other end is conduct that is clearly dangerous and abusive (such as physical violence).

The following steps[2] are to be followed only after you have determined that your husband is approachable, calm, and willing to hear your side of the issue. (If your husband tends toward verbal or physical outbursts, extreme defensiveness, or accusatory behavior of any kind, please turn to appendix B before continuing through this chapter.) If for any reason you are unsure whether a confrontation is safe, you should ask a third party to help you—whether that is a pastor, a counselor, or a mutual friend. If you are able to determine that your spouse is generally approachable, then you can move on to discussing the matter at hand.

1. Acknowledge What Is Right

Throughout history, wives have gained a reputation for being "nagging" and "quarrelsome." We see this in the Old Testament as part of the warning and instruction given in the book of Proverbs. If a wife only ever points out what her husband is doing wrong, she can wind up becoming like the endless dripping of a leaky faucet (see Prov. 27:15–16), to the point where her husband

2. Following Andy Crouch, we have used the example of Paul's letter to Philemon to develop some principles for approaching a spouse who is misusing their power, but our process and focus is quite different from his. See Crouch, *Playing God: Redeeming the Gift of Power* (IVP, 2013), 221–30.

wants to go live on the edge of the roof (see Prov. 21:9). Wives should be careful not to focus solely on their husbands' faults and failures, as this can easily lead to a critical spirit that strains the relationship.

However, that doesn't mean a wife should ignore real concerns or frustrations. A more effective way to foster healthy communication is to balance necessary correction with a genuine acknowledgment of what your spouse is doing right. By recognizing their strengths and efforts, you create an atmosphere in which both encouragement and accountability can thrive.

When you are feeling overlooked and stepped on, or when your husband repeatedly dismisses your perspective, you can and should point that out. But consider how, when writing a letter to address Philemon's misuse of power against his ex-slave Onesimus, Paul didn't start with what he noticed was wrong. He started with what Philemon had done right: "I hear about your love for all his holy people and your faith in the Lord Jesus. . . . Your love has given me great joy and encouragement, because you, brother, have refreshed the hearts of the Lord's people" (vv. 5, 7 NIV). You can do the same. Your feedback will be better received by your husband, and your heart will avoid bitterness and resentment, if you start by noticing something positive about his character, actions, or efforts before offering your critique.

By acknowledging the good, you aren't necessarily avoiding or ignoring the hurt. You are simply starting on the right foot and expressing your desire that your husband flourish. This shows that you are appealing to him on the basis of love (see v. 9) and not on that of your rights or demands. For example, if your husband is normally a hardworking provider, then express your appreciation for that before you address the way he misuses power.

2. Make a Request

The second step in addressing misused power is to make a request of your spouse. A request is an open and respectful appeal through which you invite someone to consider an action or a change. It is not a demand, which assumes compliance and works against a couple's unity, collaboration, and mutuality. Rather, requests allow the couple to discuss and mutually understand each other's opinions.

Making requests is a vital skill to practice in a marriage, especially in one that strives for mutuality. It helps to prevent one person from dominating the other, lack of clarity from resulting in false assumptions, or important desires from being unintentionally overlooked due to poor communication. Such requests can take many different forms—like asking for more help with the kids or chores, suggesting a family vacation, or imploring your spouse to seek marriage counseling. Making a request opens the lines of communication and sets a humble and loving tone.

After Paul pointed out the good that Philemon was doing, he gently and calmly made a request of him. He told Philemon that he was sending his former slave Onesimus back to him so that he might have a chance to treat him in a Christlike way. Though Paul had the authority to command Philemon, he chose instead to make a request in love, saying, "I prefer to appeal to you . . . so that any favor you do would not seem forced but would be voluntary" (Philem. 1:9, 14). Similarly, a godly wife wants her husband to respond out of love instead of out of duty.

A wife makes a request—not because she lacks power or must ask permission but because she desires a shared solution. She seeks her husband's willing participation rather than trying to force him to change or remaining silently frustrated. True restoration requires both spouses to work together, not one imposing their will on the other. Paul exemplified this in his letter to Philemon.

Instead of framing the conversation as an accusation, express your concern while offering a clear and constructive path forward. For example, if you think that your husband is making major financial decisions without your input, you could say, "I really appreciate how you work hard to provide for our family, and I know you want to make wise choices. I feel like I haven't been part of our family's financial decisions lately, and that's been hard for me. Could we set aside time to go over these things together so that I can better understand and contribute to our financial goals?" This kind of request acknowledges your husband's role, expresses your feelings honestly, and provides a specific action you and your husband can take together. By making a request rather than issuing a demand or shutting down in frustration, you bring teamwork and mutual respect into the conversation, fostering an environment in which both spouses can feel heard and valued.

3. Balance Power; Don't Overpower

How do we distinguish between actions that are justly performed and those that are unjustly imposed? Power imbalances—whether due to physical strength, authority, experience, or awareness—do not inherently entail misused power. In a marriage, the abuse of power is best avoided by ensuring that both husband and wife willingly engage in a shared decision, action, or experience—free from coercion, pressure, or manipulation. In other words, both spouses assent to the decision, action, or experience and neither feels tricked, forced, or obligated to comply. This willing assent is most critical in matters of sex and finances.

Unfortunately, certain Christian teachers have suggested, and even outright advocated for, the dominance of a husband in marital sex. They have implied that wives are bound by biblical law to meet their husbands' sexual needs, no matter what they think of their requests. Yet 1 Corinthians 7:3–5 describes sexual mutuality when Paul explains that each spouse has rights over the other's body and that they should not deprive each other except by mutual consent.

This means that a wife should never feel pressured to engage in sexual acts that violate her conscience, comfort, or convictions. If something within the sexual relationship causes her distress, shame, or pain, she has the right to say no, and her husband should respect that boundary. Moreover, ongoing pressure, manipulation, or persuasion does not constitute true consent. Husbands are called to love their wives as Christ loves the church (see Eph. 5:25), which means honoring their dignity, emotions, and boundaries rather than demanding intimacy.

Similarly, a husband misuses his authority when he is secretive about money—hiding accounts, opening credit cards without his wife's knowledge, or pressuring her into unwise financial commitments. Likewise, if he restricts household spending or enforces unrealistic financial expectations, he is exerting control rather than fostering wise stewardship. In a healthy marriage, financial decisions should be made with transparency, unity, and mutual agreement, not by one spouse wielding power over the other.

When power is misused, it creates an imbalance in which one spouse dominates the other. However, the solution is not to conquer or control in return. If your husband is misusing his power, you should seek to balance power, not overpower, in an effort to restore mutual respect and stability. Power, when used rightly, values the dignity, worth, and agency of both individuals. When you are given opportunities to approve a course of action, you and your husband ensure that his use of power is not coercive or exploitative but operates within the boundaries of love, respect, and biblical responsibility.

Paul gives us an example to follow when he writes that Onesimus is no longer a subordinate but a beloved brother (see vv. 15–16). Philemon is to think of him as an equal. In addressing these areas of consent and power, a wife's goal is not to put her husband "in his place" by elevating herself above him, nor is it to subordinate him in the process. The goal is not to establish superiority in any way but rather to establish mutuality.

You must be careful not to swing the pendulum in the opposite direction. If you respond to your husband's misuse of power by seeking control for yourself, you risk repeating the same mistake from the other side. This power struggle leads to a battle for dominance rather than restoration. Instead of reacting with force, you should slow down; seek wisdom, prayer, and godly counsel; and work toward a solution that fosters mutual respect and stability.

4. Approach Him as Your Partner

Since mutuality is a key ingredient in keeping a marriage running smoothly, you should approach your husband as a partner—not as a superior, an inferior, or an enemy—even when you are addressing a power imbalance in your relationship. You are both working for the Lord. You both have the same ultimate goals.

Paul approached Philemon as a partner (see v. 17), hoping that Philemon would be stirred to treat both Paul and Onesimus as partners as well. In the same way, a wife who is confronting her husband about misused power should do so with a heart that seeks restoration, not retaliation. Trying to win a power battle by exuding more power is completely futile—it only creates further division.

Approaching your husband as a partner requires an intentional shift in both heart and action. It starts with remembering that biblical leadership is rooted in service, not control, and that Christlike submission is about love, not passivity. A wife who desires to bring balance back to a marriage distorted by misused power must prepare her heart to approach the situation with wisdom, patience, and a genuine desire for unity. This means examining your motives: Are you addressing the issue to restore health to your marriage, or are you reacting out of frustration and a need to "win"? True partnership is built on mutual flourishing, not personal victory or vendetta.

Before speaking, it's wise to pray for a spirit of love rather than anger, courage rather than fear, and clarity rather than confusion. A spirit of partnership levels the playing field and operates according to the Golden Rule, which tells us to treat others how we want to be treated. Viewing your husband as a partner carries that same connotation—"I am treating you the way I would like you to treat me."

It's easy to lose sight of partnership when hurt, frustration, or resentment has built up over time. If a husband has misused power—whether by dismissing his wife's voice, making unilateral decisions, or coercing rather than leading—his wife will naturally feel the impulse to either fight back with equal (or greater) force or withdraw completely. Unfortunately, both responses tend to deepen the power imbalance rather than heal it.

Partnership is also lost when unhealthy or imbalanced teachings about authority take root in a marriage. Some women have been led to believe that biblical submission means never questioning their husbands' actions, leading them to silently suffer. Others have internalized the message that they must fight for dominance in order to be heard. Neither of these approaches reflects the mutuality and partnership that God intended for marriage.

As you approach your husband, take steps to cultivate a heart of respect and communicate with honesty, humility, and care.

You might say something like "I feel like my voice isn't always considered when we make decisions, and that's hurting our relationship. Can we talk about how we can work together better?" Or "I know you want to lead well, and I want to support you. But I also want to feel like my thoughts and needs are valued. How can we make sure we're both heard?" When you speak out of a desire for unity rather than a hunger for control, you reflect the kind of godly wisdom that brings life and health into even the most troubled marriages.

5. Settle the Debt

The next step in the process is to settle the debt. Paul is willing to take on Onesimus's debt himself (see v. 18). Within marriage, however, the debt you settle may simply be the sin you have contributed to the situation. Instead of pointing out your husband's wrongs, settle the debt by taking responsibility for what *you* have done leading up to this point. How have you contributed to the conflict?

For example, if you have allowed your husband's power to go unchecked because you were avoiding conflict and refusing to share your feelings, you should repent of that. This doesn't mean that he hasn't also contributed to the problem or that his contribution wasn't, in some cases, greater than yours, but it does mean that you acknowledge the part you have played and take complete ownership of it. This is an eminently biblical concept, as we see in Matthew 7:3–5; Jesus tells us to take the log out of our own eye before we address the speck in someone else's.

At the same time, settling the debt does not mean covering over or minimizing the wrong that was committed and the hurt that resulted from it. In Philemon, Paul doesn't pretend Onesimus didn't do wrong—he acknowledges it and still offers to pay the debt. This is the heart of gospel-shaped love: a willingness to suffer loss for the sake of reconciliation, even when the offense is real. If your husband has misused his authority, that is a serious issue. Scripture does not minimize the sin of using power to control or wound others. In fact, God consistently confronts the abuse of power throughout the Bible (see Ezek. 34; Col. 3:19; James 3:1). So, while you are called to own your part of the conflict, this does not require you to excuse or cover up his sin. Instead, you are choosing to reflect the mercy of Christ by engaging the situation sacrificially, not self-righteously.

But there is also a side of settling the debt that involves the perpetrator coming to terms with consequences. You can display the mercy of God while still candidly acknowledging the actual ways that your husband's choices have harmed you. In the first step mentioned above, you might say, "I want to begin by acknowledging that I've allowed bitterness to take root in my heart instead of bringing this issue into the light with honesty and love. For that, I'm truly sorry. My desire is to reflect the mercy and grace of Christ—not just in offering forgiveness but also in speaking the truth with humility. There's something you've done that has deeply hurt me, and I want to share it—not to condemn you but to pursue healing, reconciliation, and a stronger, more Christ-centered marriage."

You may follow this up with an honest conversation in which you reveal to your husband exactly how his actions have impacted you. This isn't to shame him or hurt him but to help him gain understanding and develop empathy. The conversation might continue like this: "I feel very small and insignificant when you talk for me and over me in conversations with others. I know that I am not as outgoing as you are, but I still want to be seen and heard just like you do." Your words should not be accusatory and should focus more on the impact rather than the actions themselves. Point out the particular scenario or behavior, but don't go back to it unless he voices a desire for clarification or further discussion.

Some misuses of power are ingrained habits that take time and patience to change. As in the example given above, your husband may have been talking over people since he was a kid. This might have been the way his family communicated, so perhaps he didn't even know that he was doing it or that it could be hurtful to someone else. None of that excuses the fact that he has used the strength of his voice and the confidence in his personality to overpower you. But it does mean you may have to mention it again or agree on a signal that will remind him that he is doing it. Remember that the overall goal is to allow him an opportunity to make changes on his own, not to police or parent him into making an adjustment. You are to be a helper to him—one who is patient, understanding, and merciful.

To settle the debt in this way is not to erase the wrong but to approach the wrong with a posture of redemptive sacrifice. This may look like addressing the sin with clarity and courage but without demanding vengeance or restitution. It means offering forgiveness even when your pain still lingers, entrusting ultimate justice to God while humbly asking your husband to walk the road of repentance. Sacrificial love doesn't minimize sin; it makes space for grace to enter it. As Romans 12:21 says, "Do not be conquered by evil, but conquer evil with good." In this light, settling the debt becomes an act of spiritual strength, not weakness—one that is rooted in the gospel and shaped by the cross.

6. Give Him the Opportunity to Act

Paul laid everything out before Philemon, but he never gave him an ultimatum. He didn't threaten him or use force. Paul went above and beyond to seek peace with his brother in Christ. His goal was never personal vindication. When the letter ended, Paul had basically left the ball in Philemon's court. He wanted to allow Philemon time to respond and choose to do what was right.

Similarly, when you make a request of your spouse, give him the opportunity to act on his own. You may be tempted to hover over your husband until he makes the changes you have requested. But badgering and begging can provoke even the most calm and patient spouse. Present your request, then give him time to act under the compulsion of the Holy Spirit.

The truth is that spurring on the change yourself will not ultimately give you much satisfaction. It will just leave you wondering if he would have made the choice on his own or not. At the end of the day, kind or loving gestures performed under duress don't feel very reassuring. They don't show you that he truly values the power he possesses, understands the hurt he has caused, or desires to make genuine change. And making these changes for him does not give him the opportunity to learn and grow from the situation as well.

Giving your husband the opportunity to act means truly trusting that vengeance belongs to the Lord and letting go of the need to even the score. As most of us were taught as children, two wrongs really don't make a right. At this point, you have already settled the debt with your husband, so there is nothing more for him to pay. If all the previous steps were part of restoring stability and balance to the marital power scale, then these last two steps are part of the flourishing that comes out of the hard work you put in.

Creating space for your husband to act on his own accord is simply walking the path of sanctification alongside him, taking seriously your role as his helper. Though his challenge is to go above and beyond basic growth, your challenge is to not grow weary from doing the good work of helping him become more like Christ. You have done the more immediate work of pointing out a weakness; now the rest of the process is the unpredictably tedious work of progressive sanctification. You wait, move at God's pace, and use your skills as a helper so that your husband can work to rectify the specific issue you have brought to light.

7. Commit to Restoration

The final step in addressing misused power is to seek restoration. Consider Paul's words in his letter to Philemon: "Prepare a guest room for me, since I hope that through your prayers I will be restored to you" (v. 22). Of course, in a marriage the act of preparing a guest room would be a step in the opposite direction, but in the context of Paul's relationship with Philemon, this was a commitment to restoration. A conflict had the potential to bar Paul from ever being welcomed back into Philemon's household, and so the offer of a guest room would indicate that their friendship had not been harmed.

As you give your husband space to consider your requests, consider ways to restore joy and intimacy in your marriage. Though his sin may have consequences that cannot or should not be completely overlooked, you must seek to balance that reality with a commitment to reconciliation. As you strike that balance, your heart will be oriented toward the wholeness that God intended or, in some cases, a beautiful newness that has never before existed in your marriage.

Humans do not actually possess the ability to "forgive *and* forget." Memories of harm stay locked in our minds, hearts, and bodies, sometimes outlasting even the names and faces of loved ones as old age steals our clarity of thought. While we may live with the harm inflicted by misused authority, we should also strive to live with an open heart toward whatever God might be doing as he works through our pain.

If your husband persistently refuses to engage in discussions about power dynamics, it may be a sign that you need to seek guidance from a pastor or counselor to help you soften the impression that the events of misused power have stamped on your heart. Healing often begins not with forgetting the past but with committing to follow God as he calls your heart toward truth, humility, and restoration amidst the hurt that still lingers.

WHEN YOUR WIFE CONFRONTS YOU

No one likes to be confronted, but Christians are called to correct, even rebuke, one another (see Matt. 18:15; 1 Tim. 5:20). We all need this. Husbands need this. Husband, here are several ways to respond if your wife confronts you. These will help you grow in godliness and cultivate a healthy marriage.

1. Respond with Openness

If your wife raises concerns that you have been misusing power in your relationship, try to respond with humility and attentiveness. Whether or not she begins by acknowledging what you are doing right, and even if you do not agree with her assessment, you should avoid becoming defensive or dismissive. Especially if her approach reflects both wisdom and respect, keep in mind that she is not attacking you but seeking to strengthen your relationship.

In these situations, you can demonstrate love by truly listening, asking clarifying questions, and expressing gratitude for your wife's trust in bringing the concern to you. Scripture teaches us that wisdom is "open to reason" (James 3:17 ESV). A wise person, then, receives constructive feedback. Instead of viewing her words as criticism, you should see them as an opportunity to grow, knowing that your leadership is most effective when you exercise it with integrity and care. A husband who responds with openness and a willingness to examine himself fosters a relationship in which both partners feel safe to address challenges that arise. This in turn reinforces mutual respect and shared responsibility as they seek to honor God's design for marriage.

2. Acknowledge Her Concerns

Remember that God often uses a wife's insight to correct and guide her husband (see Prov. 27:17). So, as your wife makes a specific request, do everything you can to display a deep willingness to engage in open dialogue, humbly seeking to hear what God might be revealing through her. Even if you initially disagree, start by acknowledging her feelings and affirm that her perspective matters.

For example, you could say something like "I really appreciate you bringing this up, and I don't want you to feel left out of these decisions. That's not my intention. Let's sit down together and go over everything so that we're on the same page." This kind of response reassures your wife that her voice is valued while also reinforcing the partnership in your marriage.

If you realize you have been unintentionally misusing your power, take responsibility by saying, "I see how my decisions have affected you, and I want to do better about including you moving forward." By responding with openness and a desire to work together, you not only honor your wife's concerns but also strengthen trust and unity in your relationship.

3. Honor Her with Sacrificial Love

In marriage, both spouses should have a voice and no decisions should be made through force or unilateral control.

Otherwise, power becomes oppressive rather than constructive. This is particularly crucial when discussing authority, leadership, and influence—if you are not seeking your wife's willing approval of your decisions and actions, you can easily slip into patterns of domination, coercion, or abuse.

If your wife approaches you to bring balance and stability back to your marriage, make a commitment moving forward to ask for her assent to the decisions you make. Vow in your heart never to take advantage of your wife through coercion, manipulation, or pressure but to honor her dignity, value, and worth as an image bearer of God.

Unfortunately, some distortions of biblical teaching encourage men to embrace an unhealthy, forceful masculinity—one that focuses on "taking control" rather than leading with wisdom, humility, and care. This perspective overlooks Jesus's servant-hearted use of power. Jesus honored the will of others. He never forced people to submit to him but instead invited them to follow him willingly, and he leads his church not by force but by sacrificial love. His example reminds us that leadership in marriage should be not about control but about love, service, and mutual agreement.

A husband's role is not to demand submission from his wife but to take the lead to cultivate a partnership with her, fostering a relationship built on love and honor. When power is used rightly, it reflects Christ's love—one that invites, nurtures, and honors. By embracing Christ as his model, a husband can cease to use *power over* his wife and instead use his *power under* her, to build her up in grace.

4. Pursue Reconciliation

Christ treats his bride not as an adversary but as his beloved. A husband who honestly thinks of his wife as a true partner, united to him in purpose, will listen carefully, resist the urge to become defensive, and seek to understand her perspective. Partnership means affirming her voice, not dismissing it. James reminds us, "Let every person be quick to hear, slow to speak, slow to anger" (James 1:19 ESV). You cultivate partnership when you receive your wife's words with patience and view her concerns not as attacks but as invitations to grow together. Rather than countering her critique by asserting your power, you demonstrate Christlike strength by responding with gentleness. This is a clear way to show that your leadership is rooted in love, not control.

A husband confirms his partnership by pursuing reconciliation. "Do nothing from selfish ambition or conceit, but in humility count others more significant than yourselves" (Phil. 2:3 ESV). To respond as a partner is to seek unity rather than victory, to confess sin when needed, and to work toward mutual flourishing. In this way, you embody the gospel within your marriage—demonstrating that husband and wife are not enemies on opposing sides but one flesh, joined together in Christ's redeeming love. It might help to repeat back to your wife what you are hearing her say, keeping in mind that she is not an enemy or an opponent whom you are trying to prove wrong, but rather the partner whom God has given you.

5. Repent of Your Sins & Then Walk in That Repentance

A Christlike husband doesn't make excuses for his sin or shift blame. Instead, he owns the fullness of his wrong, recognizing how his actions have hurt and perhaps even silenced the one he vowed to cherish. True repentance begins with clear-sighted confession before God and the one who has been sinned against, without minimizing the offenses or propping up self-righteous defenses. If your wife makes you aware that you have sinned against her, it is important that you acknowledge that real damage has been done.

As you respond humbly, resist falling into a cycle of shame or performative sorrow. While deep sadness over your sin is appropriate, dwelling on it too long keeps the focus on yourself rather than your spouse. It is far better to accept the real consequences of your actions and commit yourself to the hard, often slow work of change.

Your wife's pain may linger even after you have apologized and she has offered forgiveness. Honor that pain with patience and empathy, not irritation. If she gently alerts you that you've fallen back into a harmful pattern you've agreed to work on, don't bristle or defend yourself. Rather, see those reminders as invitations to keep growing into the man God is calling you to be.

As you walk in repentance, make it your aim to better grasp your wife's experience. Work to understand not just what you did but how it made your wife feel—how it wounded her sense of worth or safety in your relationship. Listen, ask questions, and seek out ways to change longstanding habits that once served you but harmed her. Your aim should be not to manage appearances but to pursue transformation from the inside out.

This kind of repentance isn't loud or self-congratulatory—it's quiet, faithful, and consistent. It reflects the humility of Christ, who did not grasp for power but laid it down in love for his bride (see Phil. 2:5–8). So too, a godly husband seeks to lay down his own power, not just in words but in renewed ways of relating to his wife, as a daily act of love and worship.

6. Take the Initiative to Serve

Now that you have been made aware of your sin and have repented before your wife and the Lord, you have a blank canvas, an empty stage, limitless possibilities for displaying to her that your heart is lovingly bent toward balancing the power in your marriage. This is the part where you really get to take the initiative.

This doesn't mean that you grovel before your wife. No, the key, moving forward, is that you act with sincere and humble consistency. This means showing up—emotionally, spiritually and practically—in ways that assure her that you are serious about changing.

For instance, if your wife has told you that she feels dismissed in conversations, start by intentionally listening to her without interrupting, affirming her feelings, and asking questions that show sincere attentiveness and care. Remind yourself that, though your ability to communicate with others might be a gift in some social settings, it is not a gift if you use it to harm or belittle your wife. In your marriage, your power in this particular area gives you an opportunity to invite your wife into conversations rather than keeping her out. You can use your outgoing personality to create space for your wife by initiating conversations about topics she enjoys and feels comfortable engaging in, rather than always steering them toward areas that naturally spotlight your voice.

Invite accountability. Check in with your wife by gently asking, "Have you noticed any difference in this area? Is there something more I could do to help you feel safe and supported?" This kind of vulnerable leadership is powerful—it disarms defensiveness and fosters trust. Change doesn't happen all at once, but humility paired with action over time creates a new relational rhythm that honors both Christ and your wife.

Remember, the aim isn't perfection—it's *direction*. Let your direction be marked by a posture of sacrificial love, where power is no longer wielded for control but offered for care. That's gospel-shaped marriage: *Power under* lifts up the one you love.

7. Commit to Restoration

A call to restoration is something sacred that cannot be rushed or taken lightly. If you have wronged your wife simply because you had the power to do so—whether through control, neglect, or even silence—you must face that reality with honesty and humility. You must recognize that true restoration doesn't just restore comfort for your wife; it restores her dignity, trust, and sense of belonging. The final resolution of this problem can make her begin to feel like the person she truly is—someone with worth and dignity, made in the image of God and loved and valued by him.

You must not expect to be reconciled to your wife without repenting of your sins or presume that your wife will be healed without your own consistent and humble change. Try telling yourself something like this: *I want to assure that a place is prepared—a renewed place in my heart—for my wife to be honored, safe, and cherished again. I know that memory doesn't simply disappear and that healing takes time, but I want to walk that path with her, fully surrendering to what God might rebuild in us—whether it's the restoration of what was or the birth of something entirely new and more beautiful.*

You may find it helpful to seek out counseling, spiritual guidance, or other accountability measures—not to earn your wife's trust back, as if it is a transaction, but because God has called you to transformation. Ultimately, your desire ought to be not just to reconcile with her but to *flourish together* in the kind of wholeness that reflects Christ through your marriage.

CONCLUSION

Though he was particularly concerned with the relationship between Philemon and Onesimus, Paul's broader intent was to teach us that, while we, as Christians, still must live *in* this world, we have to do so in a way that makes it clear we are not *of* this world. Paul wanted to help both Onesimus and Philemon learn how to use power to help others flourish and to reveal Christ to the world around them. And that is why this letter can also be applied to marriage. It models a Christlike use of power.

Confrontation is never easy. It's not easy to confront someone, and it's not easy to be confronted. Yet addressing the misuse of power is not only appropriate—it is necessary if you hope to have a healthy and happy marriage. Christians are called to correct and even rebuke one another, and that is still true even when the person who needs correction is your spouse.

Appendix B

DETERMINING WHETHER YOU ARE IN AN ABUSIVE MARRIAGE

Authority can have a hypnotic effect, and power has the potential to make people think and act in ways they would never have imagined. When a husband sees his wife as an obstacle to his desires, physical restraint and emotional manipulation start to become alluring possibilities to him. A husband who is willing to restrain and manipulate his wife will find it easier to beat and terrorize her.

In the last decade, abuse has become a major focus in churches and Christian relationships. Valuable resources have given a voice to the helpless and hurting,[1] yet pushback remains. Some pastors

1. See, for example, Darby A. Strickland, *Is It Abuse? A Biblical Guide to Identifying Domestic Abuse and Helping Victims* (P&R Publishing, 2020); Justin S. Holcomb and Lindsey A. Holcomb, *Is It My Fault? Hope and Healing for Those Suffering Domestic Violence* (Moody, 2014); Leslie Vernick, *The Emotionally Destructive Marriage: How to Find Your Voice and Reclaim Your Hope* (WaterBrook, 2013).

have expressed concern that men could be falsely accused. Yet there is no substantial evidence to suggest that this is a reasonable fear.[2]

Though it is more common for wives to be abused by their husbands, we shouldn't turn a blind eye to the ways in which wives wrongly use their power against their husbands. When a wife observes that she is able to manipulate her husband to get what she wants, she can be tempted to use her mental dexterity and her hold on his heart to leverage situations for her benefit. Once she has gained the upper hand, any attempt the husband makes to reestablish balance can be framed as a power grab—especially within a culture that, in an attempt to protect women from male dominance, has become stuck on high alert against any man who seeks to lead his wife in any way. These conditions can keep a husband fearful of trying to project any semblance of authority, which leaves the husband–wife team lacking an essential element.

Here are eleven key warning signs for a spouse to look for as they assess whether they are in an abusive marriage:

2. For example, a study by the Crown Prosecution Service in the United Kingdom found only six prosecutions for false domestic violence allegations compared to more than a hundred thousand prosecutions for domestic violence. See Alison Levitt and the Crown Prosecution Service Equality and Diversity Unit, "Charging Perverting the Course of Justice and Wasting Police Time in Cases Involving Allegedly False Rape and Domestic Violence Allegations" (UK Home Office, 2013), available online at https://www.cps.gov.uk/sites/default/files/documents/publications/perverting_course_of_justice_march_2013.pdf). Within the United States, there have not been any large-scale studies on false claims of domestic abuse. The National Sexual Violence Resource Center has found that false claims of sexual assault are in the 2–10 percent range. See National Sexual Violence Resource Center, "False Reporting," 2012, available online at https://www.nsvrc.org/sites/default/files/Publications_NSVRC_Overview_False-Reporting.pdf. We can conclude, then, that there is no substantial support to the idea that men are often wrongfully accused of abuse.

- *Criticism.* Do you feel as if nothing you do is right or good enough? Do you feel like your spouse always has something to say about how you could do better?
- *Humiliation.* Does your spouse intentionally embarrass you? Has your spouse pointed out things they would want you to change about your physical appearance? Does your spouse make jokes about you in front of other people? Do you feel a sense of shame when they speak about you?
- *Intimidation.* Does your spouse use their size to overpower you in any way? Does your husband use his position of authority to "lord it over" you in any way? Does your spouse have a "look" that is intended to put you in your place or make you think twice? Instead of calmly walking away from a situation or speaking with a controlled tone, does your spouse make it clear to you or the kids when they have "had enough"? Does your spouse ever make threatening comments (directly or indirectly)?
- *Coercion.* Does your spouse try to talk you into doing things that you have already said you don't want to do? Do they come up with subtle ways to persuade you to do things their way so that your ideas are lost in the shuffle? Do they apply pressure to make you do things that you aren't comfortable with?
- *Manipulation.* Do you walk away from arguments feeling confused? Do you feel as if your perspective is wrong, but you don't understand why? Do you feel like your complaints or concerns are being used against you? Does your spouse twist your words to mean things you did not intend?
- *Lying.* Have you ever caught your spouse in a lie (especially one that they seemed to tell for a silly reason)? Does

your spouse ever encourage you to lie for them? Or do they allow others to think you are lying when your truth doesn't match their lie?

- *Arrogance.* Does your spouse act as if their way is always best? Do they openly boast, or do they find ways to mention their accomplishments through backdoor bragging?
- *Unteachable.* Does your spouse regularly criticize authority figures? Do they act as if they could do a better job than their superiors or outperform any of their peers? Do they insinuate or outright say that they have all the answers? Do they seem to believe that they can do no wrong? Do they grow irritated or argumentative when you have a different opinion from them?
- *Controlling.* Does your spouse micromanage where you go, who you speak to, or what you are allowed to do? Would you use the word *trapped* to describe any part of your life? Does your spouse withhold access to money, transportation, or people? Or do they require that you earn things to which you are actually entitled—food, sex, sleep, time? Do they act as if they have the authority to determine how you spend your time—whether it is with them, with other people, or alone?
- *Dominating.* Does your spouse talk over you or for you? Does your spouse dominate conversation? Do they regularly make decisions without you? Do they ask for your input but then do what they want anyway? Do they change plans without your consent or undermine decisions that you previously made together?
- *Lacking empathy.* Does your spouse ignore your pain (whether physical or emotional)? Do they minimize your hurt or disappointment? Do they act as if your emotions

> are irrational or overly dramatic? Do they blame you for any pain that they have caused you? Do they constantly find a way to explain away your struggles while insisting that you recognize theirs? Do they consistently respond to your relational difficulties with pious platitudes while insisting that you take their side in any argument they have with others?

Even when abuse may seem obvious to onlookers, those who are emotionally wrapped up in the situation can be very confused. So, if any of the above questions resonate with you, it would be wise to talk to an understanding friend or spiritual leader who can be trusted to respond with caution, empathy, and wisdom.

Not only should we be prudent in navigating the boundaries of authority—where they should be placed, how firmly they should be fixed, by whom and how they are to be enforced—but we would also be wise to learn how to spot the warning signs of unauthorized or misused power and take action before it has time to destroy. Left unaddressed, misused power has the potential to cause devastating physical, emotional, and spiritual harm to individuals. It can also shatter relationships, homes, and churches while leaving black marks on the reputation of Christianity in general.

Did you find this book helpful?
Consider leaving a review online.
The authors appreciate your feedback!

Or write to P&R at editorial@prpbooks.com
with your comments. We'd love to hear from you.